GOD'S ROCK AND ROLL ARMY

GOD'S
ROCK AND ROLL
ARMY

THE STORY OF YOUNG AMERICAN SHOWCASE—
A RADICAL EXPERIMENT IN EVANGELISM

STORIES CONTRIBUTED BY THOSE WHO WERE THERE
AND WOVEN TOGETHER BY

LESLIE TURNER

© 2022 Leslie A. Turner

All rights reserved. Written permission must be secured from the publisher to use or reproduce any part of this book, except for brief quotations in reviews, endorsements, or articles.

Published and printed in the United States of America
For worldwide distribution.

Unless otherwise stated all Scripture quotations are taken from The Holy Bible, New International Version® NIV® Copyright © 1973 1978 1984 2011 by Biblica, Inc.TM Used by permission. All rights reserved worldwide.

Library of Congress Control Number: 2021952073
ISBN: 978-1-7343231-7-7 - Paperback
978-1-7343231-6-0 - Hardcover
Cataloguing data:
Turner, Leslie A.
God's Rock and Roll Army: The Story of Young American Showcase—A Radical Experiment in Evangelism

1. Oral communication-Religious aspects-Christianity
2. Christian biography
3. The Christian Life (Religion—Philosophy)
4. Christian Living—Spiritual growth

Dewey Decimal Classification: 248: Christian experience, practice, life

Front cover photo: Martin (Marty) Resch
Cover design: Leslie Turner, Jonathan Lewis
Interior design: Jonathan Lewis
Edited by Leslie Turner, Connie Kolosey, Gary Kolosey

Unless otherwise stated all photos are courtesy of Lowell Lytle and come from the Young American Showcase archive. All rights reserved worldwide.

Published by: Encourage Publishing, New Albany, Indiana
                  www.encouragepublishing.com

CONTENTS

PROLOGUE
Bartow, 1968   1

PART ONE

THE FIRST EXPERIMENT   5
    THE PRELUDE   6
    A MISSION TAKES SHAPE   12
    ON THE ROAD—YEAR 1   24

PART TWO

THE ROAD TO SHOWCASE   35
    THE AUDITIONS   36
    SHOW CAMP   46

PART THREE

THE SHOWCASE WAY   61
    MAKE IT HAPPEN   66
    TOTALLY PRO   70
    ROAD RULES   72
        The Women of Showcase   77

POSTER GALLERY   95

PART FOUR

RISK AND REWARD   123

PART FIVE

THE FRUIT 135
    THE APPOINTMENTS 136
    GROWING UP SHOWCASE 143

PART SIX

ROAD WARRIORS 159

PART SEVEN

THE QUESTIONS 179
    FAITH 180
    FUTURE 186
    FAMILY 194

PART EIGHT

THE WRAP 203
    A CALL TO ACTION 207
    EPILOGUE: GOD'S ROCK AND ROLL ARMY 210
    DO YOU REMEMBER? 213

ACKNOWLEDGMENTS 214
ABOUT THE AUTHOR 216

BONUS: A BEAUTIFUL STORY 217
    What did you do with your ticket? 220

PROLOGUE

BARTOW, 1968

1968 seemed an unlikely year to start. Bartow, Florida was certainly an unlikely place. Bartow, named after a Confederate general, founded by slave-owning cattle magnate Jacob Summerlin, and birthplace of Segregationist governor and senator Spessard Holland, would be the place to put the stake in the ground.

At the end of January 1968, media coverage of the TET Offensive brought Americans face to face with the undeniable horrors of the Vietnam War. The U.S.S. Pueblo was captured by North Korea, its crew interrogated and thrown into a POW camp. On April 4, 1968, Martin Luther King Jr. was assassinated, and the race riots that ensued during the following months cost dozens more lives and millions of dollars in damage across the country. Students around the globe protested the Vietnam War throughout the year, and on June 5, Robert F. Kennedy was assassinated. The rise of violent anti-government groups challenged a country struggling to understand its own problems, and the youth, students in their teens and twenties, seemed to be at the center of it all. Young people rose up around the world to question authority, to protest, to demand change, to express themselves through violent or illegal acts, and to embrace the growing counterculture of sex, drugs, and rock and roll.

All of these events created an urgency that made 1968 the year a young husband and father of three little children, Lowell Lytle, decide to try something that had never been done before, something extraordinarily risky, in order to recapture the hearts of America's disenfranchised youth and turn them back toward God. More specifically, he wanted to let them know the allure of "sex, drugs, and rock and roll" was nothing but an illusion, just as much as their assumptions that Christianity was far away from their burgeoning cultural identity. He wanted to show teens across America that a life with God at the center could be exciting and life changing, and could give them solid ground in an unstable and fallen world. What followed was more than two decades of a wildly effective youth evangelism ministry that broke all of the rules, slayed all of the assumptions of evangelism, and wound its way straight into the heart of the battlefield, the place where Christianity had been summarily dismissed more than a decade before: the public school system. It was an outrageous plan—an experiment in radical evangelism—and it worked.

During those years, over ten million high school and middle school students in every state in America and in every province in Canada, students who were born roughly between 1950 and 1980, had a shared experience: one day they were called from class to their school auditorium, gymnasium, or cafeteria, where they screamed and cheered their way through a rock and roll show the likes of which most had never seen. The music groups were called **Free Fare**, **Freedom Jam**, or **The Edge**, with a couple other experimental groups along the way. Students saw young men with rock star personas, iconic clothes, and wild hair, whose musical talent was only exceeded by their extreme showmanship. The dazzling musicians gave the crazed assembly of teens a dynamic performance that left them wanting more, and then offered the pumped-up audience a chance to come back in the evening for just that. Thousands upon thousands of students each month came back after school hours for an evening show, and it was there, in the final few minutes of the night, that the illusion of "sex, drugs, and rock and roll" was broken and lives were forever changed—more than a million lives across twenty-three years—and the ripple became a current that continues to roll forward to this day.

Along the way, something else happened. First one, then four, then a dozen, then many dozens of young men and a handful of women each year joined Lowell and his wife, Barb. Year after year, they fought the battle together. Within each one of them, a transformation occurred, and an indelible bond formed. This is the story of God's Rock and Roll Army, those young men and women who gave themselves wholly to this great experiment, sometimes risking their lives, always sacrificing their plans, their time, and their own will to it. This is the story of the changes each of them experienced, of the often jaw-dropping events that occurred, and of the extraordinary men and women who led them through it all. Through the following true accounts, you will get to know several of the Showcase family members who enlisted in this extraordinary experiment. Their experiences will shock, inspire, and entertain you. You may even recall seeing one of these bands come through your school, in the United States, Canada, even Australia. You may still have a poster tucked away in your closet. You may be one of the million or so lives that were forever changed.

Looking back at 1968, one cannot miss the similarity to today. Are the young people of this generation not also disillusioned toward the stalwarts of faith and country? Are they not losing hope in the future? Perhaps it is time for another radical experiment. Maybe you are the one to do it.

PROLOGUE

*A disclaimer: this is **not** a story about Christian music. That's a wonderful story to tell, and as this experiment in evangelism was unfolding, Christian music was experiencing its own explosion. But these bands never played a note of Christian music. They were Christians playing Top 40 rock and roll—"the devil's music," as many churches at the time believed. That was the extraordinary hook. And it worked, beyond all measure.*

Several key themes emerge when one reads these first-hand accounts, and lots of questions. Whether you are a leader in need of a vision, or a visionary in need of a push forward, you can glean inspiration from these pages: a number of concepts, rules, and methods for turning a group of strong-willed, egotistical individuals into a fine-tuned single unit, an unstoppable family who, together, accomplished the unimaginable. You will observe in their leader some character traits you may want to emulate. You may armchair quarterback the twists and turns that led this experiment to run its course. You may be inspired to try a radical experiment of your own. You will undoubtedly question some of the tactics, but you will not be able to deny the results.

And, almost unbelievably, it all started in Bartow.

PART ONE

THE FIRST EXPERIMENT

Lowell: Fish where the fish are.

To understand the phenomenon, where it came from, how and why it worked, you have to glimpse into the foundational experiences that informed the man behind it all: Lowell Lytle.

Lowell Lytle, mid-1970s

THE PRELUDE

Only One Life

Lowell Lytle was born in 1932, at the height of the Great Depression, in Kalamazoo, Michigan. He and his older brother, Terry, were raised in a home full of love, and where love for their neighbors was daily expressed through evangelism. Lowell and his brother were handing out Christian tracts, small booklets or cards that explained the path to salvation, at a very early age. A plaque on the wall in his home read, "Only one life, twill soon be past; only what's done for Christ will last," a sentiment that became a part of his DNA. Growing up in an environment dominated by church and revival attendance did not prevent the rambunctious boys from enjoying all the pleasures and adventures that children in that era experienced. The family often spent a week in the summer camping and fishing together, where his father taught him a lesson that would resonate in years to come: "Fish where the fish are."

Law #1: Fish where the fish are.

Lowell grew up about forty-five miles from Colon, Michigan, the self-proclaimed "Magic Capital of the World." He became enamored with magic tricks, and soon learned to be quite good at them, spending all of his boyhood earnings on new tricks and props. He perfected the art of misdirection and saw how it could be used to catch an audience by surprise. In his early teens Lowell received a book written by Edgar Bergen: How to Become a Ventriloquist. In no time he had fashioned his own "dummy" and, over the next few years, became an expert at entertaining audiences with his self-made talent. This path took him far away from his mother's dreams of ministry for her son, and ever closer to a successful life in entertainment. During high school, his life began to spiral further and further away from the values of his faith. He described this precarious period in his book, Diving into the Deep: *"I was speeding quickly away from a healthy walk with God and into a path strewn with the dangerous icebergs of pride, money, success, ego, and fame."*

In his senior year, Lytle auditioned for the 1950s version of America's Got Talent, a nationwide talent search radio broadcast called The Horace Heidt Show. He was selected to appear on the program and perform live before an audience—and he won. An accolade like this was his ticket to the big leagues—the opportunity of a lifetime. That night, he lay in the quiet darkness of his bedroom at home dreaming of all that lay ahead, when his mother slipped in and knelt by his bed, as she had done countless nights before. With his eyes closed, he listened to her fervent intercessory prayers: *"Lord, get ahold of my boy. With all his talent, let him use it for your glory."* His mother silently stepped away and closed his door, leaving him to contemplate her words. This was by far the greatest night of his life. Did she want him to give that all up? God tugged at his heart, and about an hour later he slid to the floor and opened up the cases holding his three ventriloquism figures. He spread out all of his magic paraphernalia, and with no small amount of anguish, prayed: *"God, if all of this can be used for you, so be it. If not, that will be just fine too. But I'm going to put you first in my life."*

The next morning he told the newspaper he was not accepting the entertainment contract, publicly expressing his intention to go to Bible school following his high school graduation. A few months later he began his first—and only—year at Moody Bible Institute. Lytle later transferred to a Bible college in Florida before finishing his formal education at Grand Rapids School of Bible and Music, where he met and married the love of his life, Barbara Jean Seidelman. All along the way, his understanding of evangelism—what worked, and what didn't—was growing and changing, and so was he. The most formative education on sharing the gospel did not come from his decades in church, his thousands of personal attempts, nor his formal ministry education. It came through the most unlikely of places: a sales meeting for a large group of door-to-door salesmen pitching Filter Queen vacuums, a job he recently took to support his new wife. He watched in awe as the leader used music, testimonies, and motivational speech to inspire a room full of young men to rush enthusiastically out into the streets of Chicago and spread the gospel of health, one vacuum sale at a time. This, certainly, was energy personified, and their mass fervor was contagious.

Law #2: People respond first to passion and enthusiasm.

Fast-forward to 1967. Lowell and his brother had started a Christian drive-in ministry some years before, first in Michigan, then in St. Petersburg, Florida. This ministry took a decade of back-breaking work to build, literally with their own *four hands.* As Lowell liked to say, "Money was no object, because we didn't have any." Step by step they labored together, each now with a young growing family, embodying a viewpoint that would permeate Lowell's life philosophy for decades to come: "Make it happen." In other words, do the work. Don't stop. Don't make excuses. Make the deadline. Dig deeper than you've ever dug before and find out exactly what you can accomplish. Remove "can't" from your vocabulary.

Law #3: Make it happen.

The Lytle brothers had family and friends to support them and help build the ministry, none more supportive than Les and Nadine Watkins, whose five children were also very involved in the drive-in. Two of those children, Connie and Ralph, would grow up to play significant roles in the ministry to come as well. Connie reflects on those early days:

» Connie Kolosey (1970–1980):

The Journey to Showcase

I grew up in Jackson, Michigan, where my parents were junior high school teachers. My father taught chorus and moonlighted as choral director at several local Baptist churches. One of those was Ganson Street Baptist in Jackson. This is where my parents met the Lytles in the early 1960s: Terry and Olive Lytle, and Lowell and Barbara Lytle. At that point, they would have all been in their early thirties. Terry and Lowell were getting started with the Drive-In Theater ministry at Devil's Lake, Michigan, and traveled to churches fundraising and presenting the vision of creating a place for a family outing that would include Christian-themed entertainment, movies, and music, and present the gospel. They hoped to attract families visiting the lake resort town during the summer months.

Terry, Lowell, and my father, Les Watkins, hit it off. They shared a passion for evangelism, and they also had a goofy, fun-loving sense of humor; they were creative, out-of-the-box thinkers. They were also artists, musicians, showmen, and practical jokers. My family (Les, Nadine, and five children) spent most summer weekends at the Devil's Lake Drive-In. My memories of this time swirl with a montage of swimming in the lake, sitting in dark cars watching Billy Graham movies, traditional Baptist altar calls ("I see that hand…"), making big batches of popcorn in the snack bar, Pic Mosquito repellent coils, eating fresh-made donuts, and drinking from gallon-size jugs of root beer late at night while the adults laughed and joked and counted the envelopes from people who had professed a decision for Christ, and or made a donation to the ministry. At one point during this period, Lowell, Barbara, and their young son, David, lived with us at our home in Jackson. I was about five at the time.

In April of 1964 on a Sunday evening, a huge tornado tore through Devil's Lake and destroyed the drive-in and a church down the road. The congregation was just dismissing when the storm came through, and most of the people were able to get to the basement. Terry and Lowell's father was helping people get to safety, got hit with falling debris, and was severely injured. He and their mother, Gladys, were both taken to a local hospital. My family was at home in Jackson and I remember the terrible storm and heading to our basement to wait it out. I recall the following day, all of the Lytles sitting with my parents in our living room trying to sort out all that had happened and what would happen next. A few days later, it was there that Terry and Lowell got the call that their father had passed.

After this tragedy, Terry and Lowell began fundraising and rebuilding the Devil's Lake Drive-In with renewed fervor. They also began work on a second drive-in theater on property located in Pinellas Park, Florida. My father had left teaching and started a business that imported jewelry and souvenirs that he sold to Stuckey stores up and down I-75. Terry, Lowell, and Les began to spend a lot of time traveling between Michigan and Florida. In 1968, my parents decided to move from Jackson to Pinellas Park to help with the drive-in ministry in Florida. I was in seventh grade at the time, and spent a lot of time at the drive-in property, watching Christian movies and manning the snack bar. By this time, Terry and Lowell began to have philosophical differences on the direction of the ministry. Lowell felt they needed to branch out to include other family-oriented movies as a way to bring in more people who did not yet have faith in Jesus. Terry took a more conservative view and felt they needed to stay with explicitly Christian films.

Stepping Out

Once the Florida theater was up and running, the gospel was delivered every night and, at first, it was packed all the time. During this time Lowell learned another valuable lesson. When they ran free movies, attendance was poor. When they charged a small fee or offered special reduced price nights, the line to get in would snake out onto the highway. The lesson: when you give something away, it has no value to the recipient. When you charge a small fee, a bargain rate, people would line up to get in. Money was finally sufficient to support the families, but over time it became clear to Lowell that something was missing. The ministry would only reach people who needed to hear the gospel if they came to the drive-in, and the results were dwindling. The "Filter Queen" philosophy of enthusiastically going out into the world was no longer effective here, and he and his brother began to disagree sharply on the direction of the ministry.

Law #4: People see more value in something when it has a cost.

With the operation running smoothly but the evangelistic outreach becoming less effective, Lowell's insatiable drive to point people to Jesus led him to spend more and more time working with Youth for Christ. He also helped director Shorty Yeaworth (The Blob movie series) develop a film called Way Out, which played in regular theaters as a powerful tool to reach drug addicts and help them move toward sobriety. During an era when drug use among youth was becoming an epidemic, this experience working with Shorty was transformative for Lytle, opening his eyes to the troubles around him. Lytle wrote:

> "It was the creeping corruption of morality in an entire generation of youth that now caught my attention and my heart. Clearly, young Americans were being sold a false gospel of rebellion and dangerous, self-indulgent behaviors by those who had 'won the right to be heard,' the folk and rock musicians who had become the gurus of the 'Me Generation.'"

Lowell's passion and motivation occupied his every thought. How could they reach the younger generation, turn them away from the deceptive illusions of the rising counterculture and open their hearts to the gospel? He thought about his years using misdirection and illusion to catch his audiences by surprise. He thought about his promise years before to use his gifts and talents for God's purposes, and realized he had let his unique abilities fall by the wayside. He knew that youth had, by and large, been served an illusion of the Christian life that was just as falsely uninviting as the deception of "sex, drugs, and rock and roll" was an appealing misdirection that masked the destructively high price. His mission was set. He would find a way to reach the younger generations for Christ.

Law #5: You have to earn the right to be heard.

A plan jelled, and soon Lytle would take a giant leap of faith. With his wife, Barb, and their three young children, he left the security and religious acceptability of the drive-in ministry and launched his great experiment—a one-man show that would eventually become Young American Showcase. Lessons learned as a child *fishing with his father and from his vacuum-selling days convinced Lytle he had to find a way to "fish where the fish are," to reach youth on their own turf. Young people were already gathered together every day at school. Could he somehow get into the schools? Yes and no. It had been illegal to share the gospel on public school campuses while school was in session for a number of years. Lytle came up with a plan. He put together a secular magic and ventriloquism show and presented it to schools for free during the day in exchange for the opportunity to offer a night show where he would charge a nominal fee of one dollar. At the end of that night show, he would boldly share the gospel. One hundred fifty students showed up for his first evening show—and sixty-five of them received Christ that night. He knew he had found his purpose and method. Connie remembers the early days.*

» Connie Kolosey (1970-1980):

As Lowell began to pull away from the drive-in, he took the first steps toward what would become Young American Showcase. I started babysitting for Lowell and Barbara's three children, David, Debbie, and Laura, as Lowell and Barbara began to travel, with Lowell performing for youth groups around the state. I was only 13 myself, and David was just four years younger. Debbie was 7 and Laura was 4. I would take the school bus over to their house rather than going home in the afternoons. I helped Barb clean and cook dinner and she drove me home later in the evening. Lowell was doing "Pizza Panic" shows at schools, churches, and recreation centers. Kids who made a decision for Christ would write their names and addresses on the back of their tickets and turn them in. The Lytles would follow up with mailing those kids Christian tracts and giving their names to local churches to follow up. I began helping to sort through all of those tickets and help with the mailings, not much different from the mailing work I did volunteering at the drive-in.

A friend and colleague from the Youth for Christ organization introduced Lowell to a fellow with his same passion and drive, someone who was a skilled comedian, a folk singer, and really knew how to talk to the audience in a way that got their attention. Just a few hours after being introduced to each other, Lowell Lytle and Gary Horton gave their first performance together—a combination of folk music, comedy, magic, and ventriloquism—in Bartow, Florida.

A MISSION TAKES SHAPE

Lowell: Jib the jab.

THE BEGINNING

» Gary Horton (1968-71/1978-91):

We found ourselves in Bartow, Florida, where a gentleman named Dick Erickson, who worked with me in some camps in Florida for troubled kids, had just introduced us. Lowell and I looked at each other, knowing that we had just a few hours to put together a show for a school later that day. Mr. Erickson made the statement that if Mr. Lytle and Gary Horton could get together, it might be a powerful team to protect the lives of young people in schools. Well, in Bartow, Florida, it happened.

Lowell Lytle performing a comedy bit

Gary Horton performing on his 12-string

We decided I would come out there and strum and hum a few songs and he would come out there and do a little bit of magic, then I would come back and do another song. He was also a ventriloquist, a very good one. So he would come out with his dummy (and that wasn't me at the time). We would entertain the students that day as well as anybody that I have ever seen. I would come in at the end and wrap it up, giving them a message that included the most famous news that anyone has ever received, the good news of the gospel of Jesus Christ, that anyone who by faith accepts the gift of salvation would know that they would spend eternity with our Lord and Savior.

The amazing thing about our getting together was that we had no knowledge of each other, yet when we got together we realized that we had something going here that actually worked. So, we did a few schools. Lowell would do his thing and I would come out and do mine. We played songs that we thought were equal for the time and would be appreciated by the students.

In the day shows we would cover about three quarters of a period, about fifty minutes at the most. In the night shows, we took a little bit more time. We felt that we should really entertain so that the kids would feel that we had given them the best program that we could put on, so that we could make it possible for them to want to listen to the wonderful message that we were presenting to them, which had to do with eternal life.

As we traveled, we would often stay in "no-tell motels" because the two of us didn't have much money. We would sometimes stay in people's homes. I remember sleeping on the floor in someone's kitchen. Anything that caused us to endure the pace and the travel was worth it because, in reality, we were on a mission, and that mission had to do with young people and the world in which they lived, and the problems that they faced. We worked to encourage them and the schools to stand strong about the things that we represented, which had a lot to do with what America was—and still is. It wasn't our objective to make a lot of money. We did whatever we could do to encourage students to take a good look at their lives and their future and the priorities of living in the land of the free and the home of the brave. I was so amazed and entertained by what Mr. Lytle was able to do with his magic and ventriloquism; eventually we decided we needed a group—a rock and roll band.

BUILDING THE BAND

» Lowell Lytle:
When Gary and I first teamed up, we had no musical interlude between our performances. Just DEAD AIR. On the *Johnny Carson Show*, Johnny would introduce a guest and the band would play a musical interlude for about ten seconds, which made the program flow better. I had been helping Thurlow Spurr with some events, and he agreed to have his group record some musical interludes for us. If you were in high school anywhere from the '60s to the '90s, the Spurrlows or one of their many spin-off groups probably came to your school. They were unbelievably talented and their show was top-notch wholesome entertainment with a bit of gospel at the end. They consisted of a

choral group along with a big band, all the creation of Thurlow Spurr. At the time, Thurlow was the director of music for Youth for Christ. He was also a musical pioneer, both for contemporary Christian music and in partnering with corporate America to sponsor and pay for their gigs and equipment. The Spurrlows had been performing for almost ten years at this point, but his groups had a distinctively different musical approach than ours. We had a much deeper emphasis on sharing the gospel, played more contemporary music, and of course, were very scaled down: just two guys, a guitar, and a ventriloquist dummy. No sponsorships, no fancy costumes, lighting, or instrumentation; it was time to add another member.

» Buddy Waterman (1969):

In the fall of 1968, my first year at Clearwater Christian College, I watched two unusual evangelists performing music, comedy, and magic tricks for the students. I left after their show but got a phone call from Lowell Lytle that night asking me to audition for a rock band. They had a vision to use rock and roll as a radical new platform to reach kids in the public school system.

When I carried my drums into the audition, there was a strange collection of "Kumbaya" singers with acoustic guitars and a plastic keyboard. I almost laughed. They didn't know one rock song! Finally, Lowell asked me to play a drum solo.

I had been playing in serious rock bands for over five years—opening up concerts for the Mamas and Papas, the Turtles, Mitch Rider and the Detroit Wheels, and many other famous Top Ten artists. When I finished the solo, Lowell and Gary had this astonished look and both said, "We want you!"

I dropped out of college to join them in January 1969. They were not able to put a rock band together, so it was just the three of us—"the God Squad" as Gary would say.

We traveled the state of Florida in a fairly new VW van armed with a set of Ludwig drums, two large Altec A7 speaker cabinets, and a reel-to-reel tape recorder. The tape recorder had a state-of-the-art remote control that was activated by a button attached to my bass drum. Lowell had several brass band jazz fanfares recorded, interestingly without any drums. When I played my live drums, along with these fan fares, it was a powerful introduction to each act in our program.

Lowell did an amazing magic act, including a skunk being pulled out of a top hat. The skunk always got away from him and jumped into the audience. The crowd went wild! Gary's humor took the kids into his realm of grade school stories that made them laugh until they cried out for mercy! In Act 3, Lowell brought out Henry, his ventriloquism figure. Henry was an obnoxious flirt—always trying to make it with some pretty girl in the front row. You would swear he was alive if he wasn't made out of wood. Henry's cynical sarcasm captured the crowd with laughter and always made Lowell look like the dummy. Gary Horton was gifted with a beautiful voice. We were able to get the original soundtrack from "Wichita Lineman" by Glen Campbell. Gary sang along with it while playing his acoustic guitar; I also played along on my drums. I am sure Gary would have made Glen proud.

There were days when we had no schools booked for shows. As we were driving through the rural parts of central Florida, we would "just happen" to find a school we didn't know about. We'd pulled into the school parking lot and Lowell would say, "Let's pray." We prayed that God would lead us to a Christian teacher or principal who would give us the favor of God. God honored our faith and had us meet the right person who had the authority to immediately call all the classes to an assembly program in the auditorium or gymnasium. This was life-changing for me personally. I was very spiritually immature at nineteen years old, but God used me because I was willing to use my gifts to serve Him.

We also went into many prisons. There we would ask permission to go to the exercise area where the prisoners worked out with weights. The guards went with us, and Gary would challenge the prisoners: "Who's the strongest guy in this place?" They would always point to some huge superhero that was bigger than life! Gary would say to this guy, "Here's the game plan: I'm going to get down in pushup position and Buddy's going to sit on my back. I'm going to do as many pushups as I can. Then, it's your turn, and Buddy will sit on your back. Whoever does the most pushups wins." I'm sure all the prisoners thought Gary wouldn't stand a chance. Gary could do about eight or nine pushups with me on his back. When I sat on the prisoner's back, he couldn't get off the ground! It always turned out the same way.

By this time, we would have a huge crowd watching us; Lowell would announce that one of the guards was going to handcuff him behind his back. Then Lowell announced that he would be out of the cuffs in less than one minute! The guard timed him and, thirty seconds later, the open cuffs were dangling from his fingers! At this point, they would easily accept our invitation to a show that we would perform later. Only Jesus can set the captives free, and He always showed up and stole the show. Of all the special gifts and talents that Lowell and Gary were blessed with, presenting the gospel was their forte. As we walked out of the razor-wire gates and fences, there was always the exhilaration of victory for the many souls set free that day.

» Lowell Lytle:

The three of us would work two weeks and then take off for another two weeks to be with our families. This also gave me time to earn money to support my family, and plenty of time to think about our ministry. I loved the Spurrlows and thought a lot about their operation, but I noticed the crowds drawn to their big events were not "the fish" we were looking for. They were not the young people without a strong faith, young people being pulled so strongly toward a dangerous culture, that I knew I was called to reach. When Thurlow offered me a job, a position that would have allowed me to support my family during a time of great need, I said no. Incredulous, a short time later he came to one of our simple little shows to try to understand better what we did, bringing along Stan Morris, his musical arranger.

The junior high school auditorium, which held approximately six hundred people, was filled that night. Excitement and anticipation were in the air. In the audience sat Thurlow and Stan, two extremely talented and renowned musicians, known for their professionalism and entertainment prowess. Their groups each had a couple dozen extremely talented performers, beautiful costumes and sets, lighting and sound, with live musicians and plenty of back-office support. They were about to see a guitar player that had to use a capo on his guitar, a ventriloquist who also performed magic tricks, and a drummer. That's it! I probably ought to add, Buddy Waterman was the youngest of the group, and very good-looking.

With curtains drawn, Buddy Waterman set his drums up on the middle of the stage. I was backstage stationed by the light panel, with a microphone. There were six switches controlling the house lights and one controlling the stage lights. I turned one of the house lights off. Kids started to scream. I turned the next one off, then the next one, then the next one. Each time, the kids screamed louder. Then I turned the stage lights on and said, "Ladies and gentlemen, the drums of Buddy Waterman." Buddy started beating on the drums and the kids went nuts! I started to open the curtains very slowly, and hundreds of Kodak flashcubes started going off.

Approximately 250 kids responded to the plan of salvation that night.

While driving Thurlow and Stan to the airport after the show, Thurlow sat in the front seat with arms crossed, shaking his head. "That was amazing! If you put a bass and a keyboard player with your show you will have a rock band." I wasn't too keen on that. I didn't like rock and roll. It had a "bad" image. However, if that's what the kids are biting on, I thought, perhaps he was right. I decided to think and pray about it. "I'll even let you have your pick of one of the Spurrlows," he added. Wow.

» Buddy Waterman (1969):

During Easter break, I received a letter from Uncle Sam stating that I was being drafted into the US Army. Two of my friends from high school had already lost their lives in Vietnam. I immediately went to the local Air Force recruiter. He signed me up on a ninety-day delayed enlistment. This enabled me to finish the school year traveling with Lowell and Gary into many elementary, junior, and senior high schools. In every school, we performed an assembly show and then announced we would return to do a "Laugh Out" night show. The Lord blessed and we always played to a packed auditorium. God saved His best for last when, at the end of the night shows, we shared our life-changing testimonies of Jesus forgiving our sins and making us new creations in Christ. We gave a personal invitation, and the kids responded. We asked them to tear off a part of their admission ticket and put it in a box on their way out, to let us know they received Jesus.

Spending five months together on the road opened an in-depth relationship with two guys who really knew God in ways that gave me a whole new perspective about God's character. Joy is only second to love in the list of the fruit of the Spirit. Lowell and Gary's sense of humor was always the ace in their winning hand. As we were driving across Florida, they loved to tell me hilarious "God stories" of their endless adventures. Once they got me laughing, the game was on! One story led to another, to another, until the pain from laughing was overwhelming. I begged them to stop, but that just fueled the fire. I was going to be the first human who literally died from the pain of laughing!

One day as we were driving down I-75, there was a new song playing on the radio:

> "...He's free as a breeze, he's always at ease. He lives in the jungle and hangs by his knees—as he flies through the trees with the greatest of ease—in his BVDs..." It was Ray Stevens singing "Guitarzan."

Lowell got that visionary look in his eyes. "We've got to do that song. It's going to be great for our show!" His plan was to play the tape while we pantomimed and acted out the characters of the song. The next day we rented a motel room where Lowell began teaching me about the fine art of pantomime. We got a copy of "Guitarzan" on cassette tape and I started practicing about 9 a.m. By noon I was sure I had it perfect. Lowell showed up with lunch and asked me to wow him with it. When I finished, he wasn't smiling. Then he said, "You have to make the people believe you are really singing!" He came back again at 5 o'clock and, by then, I knew I would be singing that song in my sleep.

When we finally performed it live, Lowell was dressed as a 6'4" Jane with a leopard skin, two coconut shells, and a wig. Gary came out jumping over a speaker cabinet dragging his monkey knuckles behind him. It was a hit that would continue to be used for over twenty years. On June 20, 1969, I flew to San Antonio, Texas and reported to Lackland Air Force Base to begin my four-year enlistment.

[Lowell had to find a replacement for Buddy on drums as fast as he could. He remembered a young drummer who had been part of the drive-in ministry, Wayne Hackett. Wayne remembers their first gig:]

» Wayne Hackett (1969-1972):

I first met Lowell Lytle when I was just sixteen, before Young American Showcase existed. I was a technician inside the booth of the Christian drive-in theater in Devil's Lake, Michigan that Lowell ran with his brother, Terry. Lowell invited me to Florida on spring break. We put on our first show together on the roof of an ice cream parlor.

» Lowell Lytle:

Of course, we did decide to switch to rock and roll as Thurlow encouraged, and quickly pulled together a band. We now had Wayne on drums. I asked Terry Casburn from the Spurrlows to join us on bass, convinced Joe Brown to take a hiatus from Indiana University to play keys, and Gary Horton stayed on guitar. I was the front man. During the show I still did magic and ventriloquism, so of course my vent figure, Henry, was a part of our group as well. We arranged to work up our set in Michigan, staying at my in-laws' farm.

Thurlow's manager, Stan Morris, graciously worked with us to put together our show during our first "show camp" at the Ionia fairgrounds. We were on our way. After we had started touring Florida, Thurlow came down to Miami with Stan and produced a record for us to sell in the night show. Thurlow also lent us the funds we needed for that first band's equipment.

Thurlow's advice and support that first year was invaluable, and I will always be grateful for it. Though successful for over twenty years, we never achieved the international fame and glory enjoyed by Thurlow Spurr across six decades of work. He was credited, along with Ralph Carmichael, with giving the contemporary Christian music genre its start. He had an incredible legacy that continued for many decades and changed the gospel music industry forever. Our mission, and our audience, was different; we measured our success in souls and changed lives, and we share that credit with Thurlow Spurr.

» Terry Casburn (1969-1972):

Five 45s

In 1968, I was touring as a singer with Thurlow Spurr and the Spurrlows, performing secular music at high schools across the country and promoting driver's safety. This was a twelve-voice ensemble accompanied by a fifteen-piece orchestra. It was called "Music for Modern Americans." We were very polished and well-rehearsed. We would end our performances with a few members of the cast giving their testimony. Thurlow would explain the plan of salvation and we would lead an altar call for those who would like to be saved. Many were led to accept Christ as their personal Savior and many more rededicated their lives to Him.

Fast forward to early spring of 1969. I was seated on Oral Roberts' private DC-9 plane. We were on a trip from Little Rock, Arkansas, to a performance in Tulsa, Oklahoma, where we were opening for the Beach Boys at the arena. As I was catnapping on the short flight, I felt a tap on my shoulder. I turned to notice a very tall gentleman who was probably ten or fifteen years my senior. In a very deep voice, he complimented me on my performance the night before and asked me if I played an instrument. I replied that I did not. He asked, "If you could play an instrument, what would it be?"

I said, "Bass guitar!" That was the entire conversation as I recall, and my first introduction to Lowell Lytle. The next thing I know, I'm in rehearsal camp for the next season with the Spurrlows, and somebody sets me up with bass guitar lessons from a young man named James Owenby. James was a wonderful musician and only had a few days to show me the basics. I was given a Fender jazz bass, a small amplifier, and five 45-rpm records to learn. I only had the summer to learn it, so I dove in headfirst. Little did I know at the time that Lowell Lytle would become such an influential person in my life.

I had learned a lot about hard work touring thirty-eight states the year before with the Spurrlows—or so I thought. The lessons about performance, life, and deeper spirituality were still to come.

[Terry Casburn was Lowell Lytle's "pick" of the Spurrlows that Thurlow had so generously offered. His next national tour would be as the new bass player in the first Free Fare band. Terry went on to play a couple more years with Young American Showcase. His personal experience is a good example of how the Showcase model went far beyond teamwork, far past good leadership. Terry reflected on his personal and professional growth during those year:.]

It was written that there are but a few defining moments and influential people in your lifetime. Lowell was certainly one of those people. He became my teacher, mentor, surrogate father if you will, over that first year. He instructed me on the tenets of good performance such as eye contact with the audience as well as giving your all for every performance no matter who or how many were present. He taught me about relationships with the opposite sex. We learned about working together as a team to achieve a common goal. Pretty lofty stuff for a nineteen-year-old who thought he knew it all already!

MOONSHOT

On July 16, 1969, Apollo 11 launched and began its eight-day journey to put a man on the moon. Anyone old enough will likely never forget the emotion of that event, the drama, inspiration, and astonishment, a bright beam of unifying national pride during a time when Americans were deeply divided. About 150 million Americans watched it unfold, moment by moment, hanging on Walter Cronkite's every word. These guys were up there in a tin can doing something no one had ever done before, running into all kinds of obstacles, making decisions on the fly, risking it all. The slightest miscalculation could easily cost them their lives.

One month later, in Ionia, Michigan, a small group of guys worked tirelessly and without any notice to prepare for their first year on the road, a full-fledged rock and roll band charged with the mission of effectively reaching the disenfranchised youth of the day and leading them to Jesus. If they succeeded, probably no one would notice. Cronkite would not give them a mention. If they failed, no one would die—though they did come close on one occasion.

That first year was their moonshot. The guys started out with no idea at all what they'd signed up for, because it had never been done. They would run into obstacles, make decisions on the fly, and had plenty of risk and miscalculations along the way.

Joe Brown was recruited for the first band in the summer of 1969, just before his junior year at Indiana University. In the following essays, Joe describes the first rehearsal camp, the first show, and their first tour:

» Joe Brown (1969–1972):

Rehearsal Camp - Year One (Summer 1969)

I remember the bees, but even more, the honey. It was the best I ever tasted.

We rehearsed at the fairgrounds in Ionia. After daylong rehearsals, we ate and slept at a nearby farm run by Lowell's wonderful in-laws, Ma and Pa Seidelman. Meals there were some of the most delicious I can remember, with corn and mashed potatoes. And the honey. Have I mentioned the honey? Fresh from the hive, comb still in the jar…oh my. Pass the biscuits, please.

Rehearsals were something else again. I had performed in bands for several years singing covers and the occasional original tune for crowds at various schools and venues around Louisville, Kentucky, and Southern Indiana, but never had I been exposed to the kind of showmanship expected from one Lowell Lytle, actor, magician, and showman *par excellence*.

Lowell taught us the applause cycle, where he would create his one-person audience reaction after a tune, and if you had not begun the next song or comedy sketch by the time his applause had just begun to wane, you would be met with a loud voice barking, "Dead air!"

THE FIRST EXPERIMENT

My previous band experience had been out of that mold where performers had to be cool, not too demonstrative, and rarely bestowed smiles on the crowd. Plus, as a drummer, I figured my job was to be intense, concentrating on my playing, appearing too involved to smile.

Wrong. There was a lot for me to learn that year. Smiling on stage, for me, is apparently a challenge. Lowell would yell "Smile!" mid-song. I thought I smiled a big one. Then again: "Joe Brown, let's see you smile!" I was! Wasn't I? During a break at one rehearsal, Lowell told me, "Joe, you're going to become an old man, sitting on your front porch, garden hose ready to spray any little kids who wander into your yard." After that, I tried harder, but stage presence was never my strong suit.

The first group at the Seidelman farm. Top: Gary Horton, Joe Brown. Bottom: Terry Casburn, Wayne Hackett. (Missing: Lowell Lytle)

The guy who had bucketloads of stage presence in that first Free Fare was Terry Casburn, bass player, crooner, and all-around great showman as well as a good friend. He was (still is) a polished performer, having spent a couple seasons with Thurlow Spurr and the Spurrlows touring schools for Chrysler. Aside from that, he just had that elusive stage charisma. Good looks didn't hurt, either. After shows, when we talked with students, if a young lady tapped me on the shoulder, the question was frequently "What's the bass player's name?"

We needed a name for our band, and Gary Horton came up with a great idea. *[Gary recalls the story:]*

> "In Ionia, Michigan, we did our rehearsal in the floral building of a place called the Ionia Free Fair. I loved the name 'Free Fair.' We named the band "Free Fare" because the shows we were doing were free, and the fare, the debt we all owe, was paid by the sacrifice of the Lord Jesus Christ in His death, burial, and resurrection."

Free Fare's First Show

Two things I will never forget: Free Fare's first show, and the day Danny Skidmore joined the band (more on that later).

Lake Odessa High School, eight hundred people showed up for the night show, not far from the Seidelman farm. We set up on the floor of a gymnasium, no stage, no curtain to pull as we started the opening song. We were nervous about walking out—it would be rather undramatic, but Lowell calmed us down. "Have all your instruments tuned before we go on. When I make the announcement, run out as fast as you can, plug in and count off the first song."

Run out? I don't know about the others, but if I had ever run out with my hometown band, where people knew us, we'd have been laughed off the stage. Lowell knew better. He knew the value of acting the way you wanted to be perceived. So, we dutifully ran out expecting the worst: jeering laughter and personal humiliation.

Instead, they screamed as if we were the Beatles.

Hot Cars, Long Hair, and Backlash in the Sunshine State

Lowell had promised a year of performing in Florida, so after a couple of weeks getting comfortable with the shows, we pulled out of Ma and Pa Seidelman's farm and headed south.

As part of the whole "win the right to be heard" concept, Free Fare had a decidedly different look than other Christian groups of the day. Most pursued a clean-cut wholesome image: short hair for the guys, dresses for the gals, all neatly groomed. Popular rock and roll bands instead offered a rebel, hippie look. The Beatles, Jimi Hendrix, the Rolling Stones, and Three Dog Night were big.

While Free Fare performers were Christians, we needed a look that would appeal to kids who might be on the fringe. We weren't playing churches, "where the Christians were." We played schools and wanted to appeal especially to unchurched kids.

We sported some pretty cool cars: a red Daytona Charger with 440 V-8, and a Dodge Road Runner with two surfboards on top. (We actually got to use the boards a couple times, despite playing ten to fifteen shows every week.) And, of course, we had our own poster.

That first year we bought our clothes at hippie-owned head shops in Tampa. With our longer hair and less-than-button-down clothes, we looked the part of a modern rock group. For the most part, high school audiences loved our shows—and our look.

Some Christians…well, not so much.

In a Florida diner, one of dozens where we caught meals between shows that first year, the counter waitress asked who we were, and what we were doing.

THE FIRST EXPERIMENT

Lowell explained that we played for high schools and shared the gospel to students. The surprised waitress stated flatly, "Y'all cain't be Christians."

"Why not?" we asked.

"Your hair is way too long and no Christian dresses like that."

Lowell reached into his back pocket, took out his wallet, and removed a small photo of two people. He covered one of the two and showed her the picture. "Who is that?" he asked.

She looked and replied, "That's Billy Graham." Lowell shifted his fingers, revealing the other person in the photo, standing arm in arm with Reverend Graham. It was Lowell himself. She looked at Lowell, then the picture, then back to Lowell. "That don't change nothing," she concluded, and turned to another customer.

At another central Florida diner, we had just placed our order and were waiting for our food, aware of a few whispers and not-so-approving looks from a couple of ranchers. One of them rose, walked to the jukebox, and dropped in a quarter. A moment later, we heard the strains of Merle Haggard:

"We don't smoke marijuana in Muskogee, we don't take our trips on LSD…"
"We don't let our hair grow long and shaggy, like the hippies out in San Francisco do."

Message received. The occasional rejection of our look and methods were worth it in the end. A whole lot of kids who might not otherwise have been reached began a life in Christ because of that ministry.

ON THE ROAD—YEAR 1

Lowell: We can put a man on the moon but we can't get breakfast after 10 a.m.

What were the shows that first year like? What was it like pulling it all together, or being on the road, and what was it like to be in the audience? These next few stories describe some notable scenes.

» Connie Kolosey (1970-1980):

Photo Op and a Front Row Seat

Lowell decided the band needed its own show poster, just like all the teens were putting up on their bedroom walls in those days. My dad was a serious amateur photographer. He had his own darkroom, took family portraits, and developed photographs. In 1969 when it was time for the first Free Fare poster photo, Lowell reached out to his buddy, my dad, Les, to take the picture. Lowell, Terry Casburn, Wayne Hackett, Gary Horton, Joe Brown, and Lowell's ventriloquist dummy, Henry, showed up at our house in the woods one evening for the photo shoot. They were laughing, joking, and having fun together. As a budding teenager, I thought these guys were absolutely the coolest people I had ever met.

They grouped up in front of the fireplace for a picture and broke out into the do-do-do part at the end of *Sweet Judy Blue Eyes*

Re-creation of the original Free Fare Poster

by Crosby, Stills, and Nash. Being a nice Christian girl, not up on the latest rock and roll, I had never heard it before, but I will never forget where I heard it first! I was the kid watching wide-eyed in the background, and I was thoroughly smitten.

In the early years, Lowell did a lot of brainstorming and phone-working lying on his king-size bed, propped up on pillows. Various people would lounge around and wander in and out. It sounds a little weird when I describe it now, but it seemed very natural at the time. I was thirteen years old, and one particular day was sitting in the room on the corner of the bed, listening and watching. Lowell stopped what he was saying, looked at me, and said, "You are like a cat. You don't say anything, but you are taking it all in." He was right about that!

The first Free Fare played in schools around St. Petersburg and across Florida, including my junior high school. That day, I went from being an unknown new kid (we had recently moved to Florida) to being super cool when the guys saw me and gave me a big hug in front of the bleachers full of students. That group also played St. Petersburg High School and met a group of kids who continued to follow them around to several shows. Vicky Best was one of those kids. Of that group, Vicky was the one for whom the gospel message resonated. She became a believer in Jesus through Free Fare's ministry, eager to grow in her faith through her interactions with the band.

In those early days, when the guys delivered the gospel at the night shows, it was a straight-ahead evangelistic altar call. Students who prayed to accept Jesus in response to the message were asked to write their names and addresses on the back of the show tickets. The tickets were

Barb Lytle, Connie (Watkins) Kolosey, Vicky (Best) Turnage, Mary (Dye) Weaver

collected and the students were sent a gospel tract in the mail encouraging them to get involved with a local church group. Thousands of tickets were collected, creating a major clerical task. The Lytles hired a young woman, Mary Dye, to work in the office. Soon Vicky Best was also working part-time. Within a couple of years, my babysitting job also morphed into an office job. I spent most of my time after school and weekends at the Lytle's home, or at the office.

» Terry Casburn (1969-1972):

It's guys like you that get our girls pregnant!

In 1969, music, long hair, funky clothes, and comedic youthful exuberance were, for us, merely tools to win the "right to be heard." Unfortunately, not all "believers" subscribed to our methods to win young lives for Christ. Joe Brown and I were asked to come and sing in the choir at a very large church in Southeast Florida. They needed a baritone and a bass voice to help support a choral concert that they were doing. A fellow named Ron Lentini had heard Joe and me sing at our shows and asked if we would be willing to help. His group at the time was a coed ensemble that I had heard perform, and they were good. We agreed to go and help. Once we arrived at this church, someone asked Ron to make sure that Joe and I stayed out of sight and sing from offstage due to our appearance. We agreed. Before long, we were summoned by the pastor of the church to come to his office. We obliged. The pastor began to berate our appearance, condemning our presence there at his church by saying, "It's guys like YOU that get our young girls pregnant!" Well, needless to say, we were not welcome, even though we were there to help. For us, our appearance, and our work, was radical evangelism. For that pastor, it was just radical.

As a singer, I wouldn't be caught dead lip-syncing! But, as it turned out, lip-syncing was an art form back in the day! Who knew that Jerry Lewis, Red Skelton, and both Dick and Jerry Van Dyke were all very skilled at it! Now it's shameful to be caught lip-syncing when performing live! You have already read about how "Guitarzan" by Ray Stevens came to be a part of the show. In early 1969, "Guitarzan" was a Top 10 hit; I railed at the thought of lip-syncing in the beginning because I thought it was cheesy, but that song turned out to be the hit of the show, and a great set up for the segment we called "singing to the girl." I had the pleasure of being the "patron saint" of singing to the girl. I had no idea that it would continue with many of the bands that followed in YAS over the years. [*"Singing to the girl" was just what it sounds like. One of the guys would pick a girl from the audience to join him on stage and sing a romantic song to her—a very effective way to engage and endear the audience.*]

The bottom line is this: God found a way to use our meager talents and offerings to expand His kingdom. He used flawed but energetic young men to foster other young people in their quest for happiness by sharing the good news that is the gospel of a risen Savior! My heart is full for the lives that were changed because of the vision that God implanted in the heart of Lowell Lytle. I am eternally grateful for the continued spiritual leadership of Ranger Gary Horton. I will always feel a kinship with my brothers in Christ, Joe Brown, Wayne Hackett, Danny Skidmore, and all who came after.

THE METHOD

» Gary Horton (1968-71/1978-91):

As our group grew, our objective and our method stayed the same. We would entertain the schools with an assembly program and then schedule another show in the evening, that night or a day or two later. We poured out our hearts into these young people. Then I was given the privilege, I mean the greatest joy, of tying it up at the end of the show, and giving them the message that we felt was the purpose for our entire organization and our performance. We were careful not to use fake traps and gimmicks that evangelism of that day usually included. It was my honor to be able to make it as clear as I could that they should come to the knowledge of our Lord and Savior.

We played the songs that were relevant to the kids in the late '60s, and we did the best we could to be as professional as possible, to let the youth know that they mattered, and that we were honored to be able to speak to them. My contribution through playing and singing was the best I could do. It was not my destiny and I wish I could have done a better job on many occasions, but we banded together and put on a pretty good show, especially at night. This involved not just music but also entertainment with skits and other things in the name of entertainment. The thing that I love the most was knowing that we were drawing the kids that needed the message.

» Joe Brown (1969-1972):

About mid-way through the first year, the band added a white soul singer named Danny Skidmore, who had been sort of a B actor with credits on *Flipper* and some other TV shows. But his real talent was singing R&B—funky R&B, to be more precise. With a dance style beyond energetic, the man was a dynamo on stage. He definitely had the moves for the grooves. His rendition of Wilson Picket's "Midnight Hour" was great fun to see and hear, and even more fun to play. Free Fare got funky for the first time, and it was a gas.

When Danny joined us, the band changed considerably. I had never played funk as a drummer (how could that have been?) but Wayne Hackett was a huge fan, so he took drums on many of those numbers while I played keyboards. When I did play on one of Danny's numbers, I learned a world about how much fun it is to play the genre, and have been a bigger fan ever since.

[All of the members of the first Free Fare were White, but with this new influence of soul, R&B, and funk, the band was perfectly poised for a situation they never anticipated—coming face to face with the Klan.]

POLICE ESCORT

» Terry Casburn (1969-1972):

Gary Horton was the ultimate communicator. He was a spiritual warrior like none other. Turns out, he was a real world warrior as well, after his tour as an Airborne Ranger in the years that followed. I know he never backed down from a challenge. We were scheduled to perform for a high school audience in a northern Florida city that I will not name.

We had just pulled up and some young man placed a printed racist circular under the windshield wiper of our car. There were several young men placing them on all of the cars parked nearby. Gary confronted the young men after seeing the derogatory statement on the flyer and asked him what he thought he was accomplishing. I do not recall the young man's response but I do remember Gary's comment to him. He said, "We all have the right to be here. We shouldn't try and snuff out the light of another person's candle just so ours can shine a little brighter." During our daytime show at that school, Gary took extra time to explain what that meant to the audience.

[The editors love the gentle way Terry talks about Gary's speech to the student body and his politeness at not naming the city. This incident occurred in Port St. Joe, Florida. Lowell retells this event in his book, Diving into the Deep. *Following is a portion of Lowell's account, with additional background information.]*

» Lowell Lytle:

Today, I'm sure, Port St. Joe must be a wonderful city that embraces every culture, but back then, in the late 1960s, it was a town much like every other small southern town—thick with racism and conflict. When we arrived at the high school in Port St. Joe, the principal took us into his office, pulled out a drawer in his desk, and showed us some knives and chains he had there. "This is what some of the kids brought to school today..."

The backstory: The band learned that the Black students were boycotting the school because no Black student was chosen to be on the cheerleading team, so they would be playing to an all-White audience. Normally, Gary would have a slot in the morning show for a ten-minute comedy routine. He started by saying, "I see you ran all the Blacks out of the school today." The students cheered and clapped as Gary waited, then resumed with a commanding voice: "I didn't mean that as a compliment! What's the matter with you people? This is the twentieth century. You should be ashamed of yourselves!" Gary continued his passionate dress-down for his full ten minutes. He certainly engaged the element of surprise that day. Imagine the band having to come back on stage after that and continue to play their hearts out!

»Terry Casburn (1969-1972):
Many appreciated the stance we took that afternoon but the nighttime performance was a completely different story. Students as well as some of their parents showed up for that show. We had no sooner struck the opening chord before some in the crowd picked up homemade picket signs. Some read "Free Fare Unfair." Others read "Laff Out Get Out." They attempted to shout us down that night but we did our show and attempted to communicate with those that wanted to hear. Ultimately, we had to have state troopers escort us out of town after the show.

The rest of the story: The state troopers were called in because the Ku Klux Klan showed up and picketed outside the school while eight hundred students were inside watching the show, but not before burning a cross in the section of town where most African Americans lived. Pouring love and energy into the show that night was never more important, nor more difficult. Setting an uncompromising tone fortified the band's testimony. Undoubtedly, those students saw an unflinching portrayal of Christ's unfailing and courageous love in this all-White band of brothers who dared to cross the line and stand up for what was right. During the meet and greet after the show, some KKK members found their way inside and marched up and down the bleachers with vile, racist placards. And, yes, even with a police escort and quick exit, the band's amazing stand that day under Gary's tough speech was sure to have been life changing and emboldening for those students.

CUTTING A RECORD

»Joe Brown (1969-1972):
After our evening shows, in addition to having posters to sell and sign for students, Lowell thought it would be great idea to have a record, at least a single, to sell as well. We were so busy doing shows that there was little time to record, so Lowell had tracks cut in Detroit on a tune written and arranged by Stan Morris from the Spurrlow organization. The two-inch multi-track tape was shipped to Lowell, who found a couple of hours at Criteria Recording Studio in Miami so we could record vocal overdubs.

I will never forget walking into that studio during a break in their primary client's schedule. There were all the instruments set up with microphones everywhere and the typical studio accouterments (I later had my own recording studio in Louisville, Kentucky). I looked at the kick drum where most bands had the band name stenciled during that era and saw the name, "Rascals." Wow. We were doing vocal overdubs in the same studio where the Young Rascals were recording their newest album. They were on a break, leaving the room free for a couple hours, enough time for Free Fare to record vocals for the single "Baby I Love You" and the B-side, an arrangement of "Born Free."

Later, during a break in our own vocal overdub session, who walks in to give us big hugs? Lulu, who had been across the hall recording an album in Criteria's Studio B following her hit single, "To Sir with Love." For a young kid in his twenties who had played only in cover bands and college folk groups, I was star-struck.

"Baby I Love You," performed by Danny Skidmore (Lowell, Terry, Gary, Wayne, and me on back vocals), later was pick-hit-of-the-week on the Tampa/St. Pete top 40 station. We were pretty excited hearing ourselves on a big top 40 radio station. We felt we had hit the big time.

[Over the years, various bands cut many more singles to get airplay and sell at the merchandise table, a great way to raise the level of the illusion.]

DOWN TO THE RIVER TO PRAY

Lowell: Comedy is based on tragedy.

»Terry Casburn (1969–1972):
In the fall of 1969, we were tooling west across a Florida state highway in the middle of nowhere when, suddenly, the CB radio began to crackle. The message was garbled and difficult to understand at first. Then, more clearly, we heard Joe's voice. "Come back! Come back! We've had a wreck!" His voice was frantic and very high pitched for a baritone.

I was in the car with Wayne, who was driving the 1968 fire engine red Dodge Daytona Charger with the surfboard rack on top, carrying a custom-made surfboard, with the name "Free Fare" stenciled on it. We were heading toward the town of our next gig, or "Laff Out" as they were called. After hearing Joe's pleas, Wayne suddenly slammed on the brakes and pulled off a perfect "J" turn to reverse course. This maneuver would have made Starsky and Hutch very proud! Wayne put the pedal to the metal to go back and help our Free Fare brothers, who had been trailing us for several miles in the lime green Plymouth Super Bee, which was pulling our equipment trailer. We had no idea if anyone was injured or killed.

»Joe Brown (1969-1972):

I really do not remember precisely where we were, the number of the highway we were on, from which town we had left, or the name of the one to which we were headed. But the mind's image of that day is crystal clear.

We were near Orlando—that I remember—and not far from the construction location for Walt Disney's dream park, Walt Disney World. As Wayne approached an expressway on-ramp, he called on the citizens band radio we used to communicate while on the road. He needed to tell me that the on-ramp had a tight turn, and that I should slow down to take it with the trailer. "Hey Joe," Wayne called.

I reached for the CB mic, which should have been hanging in its place on the dash, but the mic was not there. I glanced to the floor and saw it had slipped from its holder, and now lay nearly under the front seat. Reaching for the mic to answer Wayne, I took my eyes off the road for a moment—long enough for the trailer wheels, with a wider wheelbase than the Road Runner, to ease off the pavement and onto the shoulder. The shoulder was either loose gravel or dirt, but in any case, a much different texture than the pavement. The trailer lurched to the right. I compensated. Then back to the left, even farther. I was beginning to lose control.

In normal conditions, with a straight road, I might have been able to slow gradually, get the trailer under control, safely stop the car, check for any damage, and then continue on our way. However, this stretch of road had something different: a drainage canal from the Disney World construction area passing underneath. We were about to cross a concrete bridge with a buttress on the side that was raised about two and a half feet, immediately ahead of the point where I began to lose control.

After swerving right, then back left, the trailer made its final yaw far back to the right, pulling the car sideways in the road. A split second later, the equipment trailer hit the bridge, ripping it from its hitch. The Road Runner continued to slide down the road sideways a few seconds, which seemed like an eternity. Miraculously, the Road Runner did not flip.

After coming to a stop sideways in the road, I asked if everyone was okay. They were. As we began to shake off the terror and the adrenaline, I reached for the radio to tell Hackett we'd had an accident.

Stunned but unhurt, we opened the door and got out of the car to check on the trailer and its contents. The trailer, or rather, its twisted frame, lay wrapped halfway around the concrete side of that canal bridge. The sides, top, and eighty percent of the contents lay strewn about the bank—and in the water—of the Disney World drainage canal near Kissimmee, Florida. My drums—my own Black Diamond Pearl Ludwigs—lay crushed in their canvas cases in the canal itself, the hard-shell trap case nearby. Our amplifiers, PA system, guitars, and many of our show clothes lay ruined in the water of that canal.

In a few minutes, the others arrived in the Daytona Charger, everyone in shock at the crushed and submerged equipment below. Clearly, even in our make-it-happen culture, we were not going make our next gig. Nor the one after that, nor the next.

» Terry Casburn (1969–1972):

As we approached the crash, we saw headlights shining in an odd direction through a fog that seemed to cling to the ground around the area of the crash like my grandmother's blanket. It was a very eerie scene as we rolled up to see the carnage. Ironically, the Super Bee was intact and sitting askew on the road, but the trailer it was pulling was gone! Praise God no one was injured. It surely could have been much worse.

The trailer was a small snow-mobile trailer that was apparently not constructed to survive a steel-reinforced concrete bridge at sixty miles per hour. As we peered over the edge of the bridge, we noticed that the trailer's sides had come apart like a five-sided cardboard box that had been unglued in an orderly manner. It revealed a pile of clothing in the center along with various and sundry other items, including our underwear! I watched as our Altec Lansing A-100 PA speakers bobbed up and down in the river and flowed out of site. My gray metallic, rolled and pleated Kustom bass cabinet was immersed in the muddy river also, along with most everything else. We were able to recover some instruments and clothing—but I digress.

» Joe Brown (1969–1972):

We called Lowell. I do not now remember who made the call; and Lowell was terrific.

Somehow, someone found a home in Kissimmee where we could stay for a few days. The days following the accident are a blur for me now. There were tears, laughter, and prayer. Lots of prayer.

Lowell called Manny's Music in New York City to order all new equipment. Lost clothing was replaced.

However, something inside me was not yet healed. After all, I was the one driving the Road Runner. I was responsible for the accident, and felt terrible. My glancing away had caused the loss of nearly all our equipment, the economic loss of several shows, and the replacement of many expensive instruments. I was feeling pretty sorry for myself for quite a while.

What I failed to see through all my own self-pity was God's grace. It was there, but it took me a while to get my eyes off myself and back to where they should be. Once I did, grace became evident. No one was killed, not even injured. There might have been oncoming traffic in the other lane with nowhere to get out of the way, but no other vehicles or people were hurt. Our car did not flip. Had I swerved a bit more, it might have been all of us in the canal, rather than just replaceable material things.

So many far worse things could have happened. But they didn't.

That is grace. And I am still grateful, more than fifty years later.

As the years went by, there would be plenty of other road incidents and dangers, but this first one was the hardest. With no margin, no backup plan, no home office to call, no other bands to lean on, no money, no spare equipment, this first band had to bootstrap and duct tape their way through, not only logistically, but physically, emotionally, and spiritually, as Joe so honestly described. A tin can on the moon.

PART TWO

THE ROAD TO SHOWCASE

Lowell: Fabricate reality.

The first band started with just one man with a calling, a huge vision, seemingly limitless passion and energy, a wife who supported him in every possible way, and God's blessing. Oh—and three small children. Now, they had a powerful, effective, and talented group of musicians who loved the Lord and were working hard at the mission, despite their setbacks. Lowell, Barb, and the band were all just making it up as they went along. Soon into the first year, the band's success leading young people to the Lord affirmed to them that they were on the right track. It also created a wonderful problem. One band could not possibly cover enough territory; it was time to scale up the organization.

YAS recruitment poster

THE AUDITIONS

Lowell: It's rock and roll, man, skull and crossbones!

Free Fare went from one person, to two, to five men on the road and four women in the office giving their all to change the trajectory of about 15,000 young lives that first year. One band became two, then four, and quickly up to eight bands a year toured the United States and beyond, powerfully sharing the gospel with upwards of 200,000 students every year, over two decades. Organizing such an endeavor, ensuring every band was trained and ready, consistently giving their best, growing, maturing, and properly managed, equipped, outfitted, and scheduled, was a monumental task. The logistics alone were staggering, and the preparation intense. The message at the end of the show had to be consistent with each band member's actions, performance, behavior, professionalism—all of it. The band members' demeanor had to be authentic—no amount of talent can make up for a band member whose faith experience was inconsistent with their message. Teens were more than able to spot a poser; if the band members were not the "real deal," if their behavior did not genuinely reflect Jesus, they would lose the audience, and the mission would fail.

There were other obstacles. Where would the talent come from? Who would prepare and manage them? Who would book the shows and accommodations? What about equipment, vehicles, props, and show clothes? The tours would ultimately be self-sustaining, but how would they pay for all of it initially? What about bookkeeping, paying the band members, managers, and staff, budgeting, planning, and paying the bills? What about follow-up? Response cards were the measure that the work the bands were doing was successful; each of those cards represented souls needing more information, needing to plug in to a local church, and more. At first, all of the administration happened at the Lytle's dining table, coffee table, and every other corner of their home. Lowell and his wife, Barb, along with a growing army of committed helpers, successfully executed the most dramatic experiment in youth evangelism in history.

As for finding an army of young men with genuine musical talent who loved the Lord, had the right personality and maturity, and who were available to sacrifice perhaps years of their lives and everything they thought they knew about performance, evangelism, and ministry, to a man, each one has a story about how they came to Showcase. Some are predictable, but many are nothing short of miraculous, reminding all who were there about the hand of God in their lives. Following are some stories that capture what band members went through on the road to Showcase:

» Paul Turner (1976-1978):

A choice - 1976

In 1975, I graduated from La Sierra High School mid-term because I just could not stay awake in my first period social studies class. Later I found out that nobody else could either. I was working late at night at a popular restaurant in town where everybody had to audition and entertain as part of their job, whether as a waiter, host, or bus boy (which I was). While there I met a couple of guys named Bill Fairfield and Dan Groves, who both said they were going to be leaving to join some kind of traveling Christian musical experience out of Florida. They thought I would be interested in doing that as well. By the time I got serious with that "Showcase" notion, I was playing drums for "the" band in town, doing big shows. Why would I want to leave that for the unknown? The band had songs on the radio, a house, a bus, and I got a regular salary, but they also had stuff going on that I was not comfortable around, as many pro bands did—alcohol, women, marijuana, and so forth. I knew from my upbringing that I had a choice to make. So, I sent in my application with my cassette tape to see what would happen. I got a call from a guy named Lance Abair and we talked a long time. Before I knew it, I was on my way to the Pensacola airport.

[Among many other things, Lance Abair was in charge of recruiting new band members, but also filtering out hopefuls who were not a good fit. Most Showcase members had to get through Lance to have any shot at joining Young American Showcase. He was often the first and only person to hear their audition tape or speak to them by phone. Like everyone else, Lance has his own amazing story, which you will find later in the book.]

» Ross "Rosco" Cooper (1973-1978):

Farley Flu - 1973

In 1972, I moved with my family to Denver, Colorado, as my father had just declared bankruptcy. His long-time clothing store chain had gone under. He could not compete with the new trend in retailing—malls.

There I was, a senior in a new high school, unprepared to make the adjustments necessary to fit in. So, I didn't. I just went about my business as I looked forward to graduation in June of '73. One day, I heard there was to be an assembly program in the gymnasium during the last period of the day. I was happy to hear this. I thought I would simply go home, and nobody would know. I remember thinking I should at least look inside the gymnasium to see what was going on in there. That's when I saw what looked to be a rock band getting ready to play. Everything was set up and the gear was impressive! I decided to stay to see this band play.

After the show, I walked up to the guitar player in the band (Mike Farley) and introduced myself. I told him that I played guitar, and Mike then handed me his guitar and said, "Here. Play." He took notice of my playing and invited me to come back early the next night. The following night, I was the first person to show up at our school. One of the band members then handed me a part of an amplifier and pointed to where it should go. I was taken aback. Why would I do this? Nevertheless, I thought it would be generous of me to help, so I placed the amplifier where it was supposed to go. That's when I got another piece of equipment with an instruction regarding where *it* should go. I was a little insulted that they apparently only asked me to come so I could set their stuff up for them. Now, here's the crazy part. If you don't think this could happen, it did—just like this:

Larry Marco (front man and bass player) came out in the audience and sat next to me. *He asked me if I could play guitar in place of Mike Farley that night.* Mike was *very* sick with the flu and could not even stand up. If he were even to attempt playing, he would need to play sitting in a chair. I told Larry, "Yes. I'll be happy to play in place of Mike Farley." I was ready to go, except for one problem. I didn't know any of the songs. But, what the hey! The show went on and Mike sat in a chair off to the side of the stage. I waited for someone to call me up, but it never happened. The show was good, and the audience responded positively. In the end, I was relieved I didn't have to watch the bass player's fingers to find the right key to play in.

After the show, I went to find Mike Farley. He was in the front of the truck resting—still sick. He and I talked for a long time. The focus of the discussion was about eternal salvation. That conversation changed my life from that point on, even to today. After I heard the gospel message very clearly from Mike in the truck, I was invited to visit with the group the following night after their show. *Long story short,* Larry Marco handed me a business card and told me, "If you ever need a job, call this number." I then put the business card in my wallet.

Soon after graduation, and within the course of a week, I lost my band, my college plans had changed for the worse, and I thought my life was over at seventeen. No hope for me. I'm a goner. That's when I took out my wallet and checked for that business card. My hand was shaking to see if it was there. And… it was—a little worse for wear, but it was there, intact. I felt saved from a life of "no hope." I called the number—long distance.

[In 1973, "long-distance calls" were a real thing, and very expensive. For young hopefuls like Rosco who had no money, just making that call presented a challenge. Rosco eventually spoke with Lance, and played his guitar audition live over the phone. Lance asked him to send in a photo. Later, he spoke with Lowell, who eventually invited him to show camp (aka "rehearsal camp"). After a twelve-hour layover in Chicago—sleeping on the floor by the departure gate cuddled up with his Jimmy Page Les Paul, an abrupt introduction to Florida humidity and a painfully hot, long ride to the New College campus where show camp was held—Rosco Cooper had arrived.]

The first person I saw when I arrived at show camp was Lance's wife, Linda Abair. I remember saying to myself, "I'm going to like this place!" I was ushered into one of the practice rooms at New College and, low and behold, my Marshall stack was set up and ready to go. It looked like a castle. I was soon introduced to some guys who looked like rock stars (Dave Sheirman, Steve Thomas, Dave Anson, and others) and someone suggested we should jam right then. I was so exhausted, I could barely keep my eyes open. I got my Les Paul out of the case, plugged it in, and started playing with them.

Then…I remember people laughing. I could not believe it! Were they going to take me back to the airport and send me home? Then almost everyone who was watching left the practice room, and came back in with another guy who looked like a rock star. They asked me to keep playing. This guy left; the rest stayed in—and kept laughing. Afterward, it appeared things went okay. I would not be sent home—not yet, anyway. The possibility of being sent home was a constant threat for me, however. I was always worried about it. I saw other guys sent home; it was always shocking and sad. At that age, being sent home would have been a sign that something was wrong with me—that I was not good enough.

[A number of other band members expressed this same fear—which was the intention. The limited number of rookies who were invited to show camp each year were told they had to purchase two tickets in order to come—one ticket in, and a return flight ticket in case they didn't make it through. How else do you get typically over-confident young musicians to try their hardest and set aside their egos to work together? A clever strategy—but not easy for young men like Rosco with limited financial resources. Rosco displayed many "make it happen" traits in his journey to Showcase. In the next story, Dave paints a vivid picture of what it

was like to go through the process from first getting that business card to making it to show camp. This story also helps us understand part of the Showcase method of careful selection, the built-in understanding that expectations were the highest possible, and success was not guaranteed. This story makes the editors wonder how many guys never found the courage to pull that card out of their wallet and make the call.]

» Dave Walker (1983–1991):

Card in the Wallet

It was my senior year in high school in the Shenandoah Valley of Virginia, a very tight-knit community of mostly farmers and fruit trees. I was in the only rock band in our school and one of only a few in the whole county. Needless to say, we were a pretty confident bunch.

One spring day our principal, Mr. Hutton, calls all of the band members down to meet him in the office. Obviously, we were a little apprehensive, but made our way to see him. As we were walking down the hall, we noticed a poster that said, "Free Fare, the band from Florida" was having a concert at our school. We joked that it was probably the US Army band because they always came to our school. Mr. Hutton greeted us at the office door and said this band was here to do a preview concert and we need to rustle up another eight to ten students to help them set up. Once again, we joked about how bad this band was going to be as we assembled the team and headed off to the gym to meet the "band from Florida."

As we walked into the gym, the door flies open and these rock stars come bounding in and quickly assemble us to set up the stage. The next thing I knew, they were sound-checking "Tom Sawyer" by Rush and my jaw hit the floor. I could not wrap my head around why this was happening. Soon the school filed in and the band came running out, ripping through a show that lasted forty-five minutes, but felt like forty-five seconds. Then we took it down and they were gone, but before they left, they told us they would like us to be the stage crew at the concert the next night.

I could hardly sleep that night, waiting to hear these unknown rock and rollers again, who were the best I had ever seen. The next day in school that's all anyone was talking about: Free Fare. I felt special to be on the stage crew.

So the band arrived, and we set them up as before. It seems the whole school has come back to see them. I cannot remember much of the show, other than when Marty (the guitar player) talked about meeting after the show to fill out an audition card for a company called Young American Showcase. Then they played a few more songs and stopped again to give a testimony of their belief in

God. This was a turning point for me, as I was a preacher's kid and now these rockers were affirming my faith, and I was witnessing my friends taking notice.

The concert ends and Marty, after signing posters, makes a call that all who are interested in Showcase meet at the end of the bleachers. About ten guys follow, and I chuckle to myself as most of these probably can only play the radio. Then Marty gives a quick pitch and hands out some business cards, but runs out by the time he gets to me. He then shakes hands with the others and tells me to follow him to the truck. On the way, he encourages me to try out and then hands me a business card. How special I felt! I got a personal business card from my new rock hero! The band members shake our hands and we watch as the truck leaves. I pull out my card to show off to the others, and the seed is planted in my mind that I will be the new member of Showcase.

For the next few weeks, I would pull out that card and hear the words of Marty ringing in my ears to call or write and request an audition packet. I eventually do, and a few weeks later, it arrives in the mail. At first, I could not open it, leaving it sitting on the kitchen counter for a few days until finally I gained the courage to take a look. It's amazing how we let the Enemy feed into our self-doubts.

So there it is: a list of songs to learn, and personality questions to answer. The request to share what it means to be a Christian. I tracked down the songs and learned the parts, but the old devil whispered in my ear that I would never have a chance, and that was it. I closed up the envelope and tossed it into the trash. How crazy was I to think this would be a reality? I put Marty's business card in the back of my wallet, where it would hide for the next year.

That fall I would start college in Lakeland, Florida, at Southeastern University. The first few weeks there were lonely. Here I was with no direction, kind of floating through life, waiting for a sign. One day I was walking by the music rooms and I heard this rock band playing without a bass player, so I stuck my head in and said, "Do you guys mind if I grab my bass?" They were cool—and a new direction had come my way. We practiced almost every day for the next three months, and after Christmas, we had scheduled some concerts. When we returned after Christmas break, our guitar player was not there. I asked, "Where is Freddy?"

I heard the words, "Oh, Freddy joined this Young American Showcase thing!" That was the moment when my life changed forever! I immediately thought of the card in my wallet that had been untouched. I went to the pay-phone in my dorm and call Showcase! "How dare they steal my guitar player?" I thought. I wasn't nervous, nor did I hesitate as the voice on the other end said, "Showcase." Immediately I rattle through my history, sounding like a nut job I am sure, and the voice says," you will need to speak to Lance Abair, please hold."

It is during that hold time that, again, the voice of self-doubt whispers in my ear to hang up—no harm, no foul. Just then, Lance picks up. "How can I help you?" he says. Once again, I stumble through the history, and then Lance stops me and says, "Hey, you are only about an hour from St. Pete and maybe you can come into the office."

I say, "That's a great idea!" and we set up a time the next week.

That week flies by and now I am on the road to Showcase. I nose around the office and find the right door, and this energetic man named Lance tells me to have a seat. Driving back to Lakeland, I cannot recall all that he said to me, but I do know that, someday, I will be a part of YAS.

Now the journey really begins. I've got to get through the next five months until the next tour, never thinking I also have to pass an audition. School finishes in May and I tell my parents that I am not returning, but joining this Showcase thing. Now, my parents are both preachers, and I am now telling them that I am going to play rock and roll for a living, and by the way, tell kids about Jesus. At first, they were a bit confused, but they must have seen the passion in me and decided to support this journey.

At the end of May, the audition package arrives (again) and I tear it open and immediately go through the songs and the questions. I finish my tape audition in a few days, in my head deciding this was a mere formality, because I was going to be the new bass player in Showcase. I told my high school friends. They never laughed in front of me, but I could tell they were not as confident as I was.

I mail the tape and I head off to work for the summer at a camp in the mountains of North Carolina, not far from Billy Graham's home. I call in to the office to make sure my package arrived, and am assured that it had, and someone would "let me know."

I wait and wait. It has been almost a month and not a word. I continue to wait. It's almost the end of July now; show camp starts in August, and my confidence level is now struggling a bit. I have told *everyone* that I will be in Showcase. So, I make another call to the office. "Showcase," I hear on the other end. "I need to know travel arrangements," I tell whoever will listen. "Please hold." Soon another voice is on the line—his name is Brent. "Hello," he says in a stoic voice. It throws me for a second. I ramble through a year and a half of my journey and Brent says they are reviewing all of the auditions. He hangs up, and for a second, fear and doubt come over me. I head back to my dorm and pray, "God, You have set this up, and I know You didn't put me here for this to end. Amen!"

A few days later, the intercom rings my name and says that I have a phone call in the office. I sprint like an Olympic athlete. Out of breath, I pick up the phone. "Hello!"

"Hi, Dave." I hear Brent's voice on the other end. "So, we think you have got the personality to do this, but we need to make sure you can play; can you send us another tape playing these songs?" He calls out "Sharp Dressed Man," "Tom Sawyer," and "Every Breath You Take."

"Of course," I say. Now, let me set the stage. I am working at a summer camp, in the mountains. There is no recording equipment, and I really do not have a lot a free time, as I am responsible for fifteen teen campers, 24/7. I have just told Brent, "Sure I can do this!" So, I learn the songs on an acoustic guitar. Now the tricky part. How can I record it and in the middle of the night when everyone is sleeping? I rig two boom-boxes and a stereo cable that is not plugged in all the way, and somehow I pull it off. It doesn't sound the best, but I give it my all and then package it up and pray.

Now, by this time it's July 31. My parents and everyone I know are asking me when this "Showcase thing" starts. I confidently say, "Soon, in the next week." The reality of this situation hits me. I have to know NOW! The next few days are tough, but my faith remains strong. God, You have brought this Showcase in my life for a reason; this is my PATHWAY!

I am on the softball fields when, echoing through the woods, I hear my name on the intercom, telling me to come to the office for a phone call. I am shaking by the time I reach the phone. This is it! My destiny! "Hello," I pant.

"So we are gonna invite you to camp," Brent says. "We have two spots available and we are going to bring four of you down, so make sure you buy a roundtrip ticket." I hold my hand over the receiver and scream out! "That sounds great, Brent."

It was summer of 1983. I never bought a roundtrip ticket. I was not going home—I was a member of Young American Showcase!

[Some musicians auditioned with bands they met on the road, and joined groups already touring who had an unexpected spot to fill. These road warriors had to learn their parts, find their place with the other guys, and learn the "Showcase way" without benefit of show camp, which could be a challenge. The following audition story illustrates the point that Lowell and Lance were not just looking for showmen and musicians. If they found someone with the right spirit, the right attitude, who would fit well in a particular group, almost everything else could be taught. They were willing to take a chance. Some musicians found their way to Showcase by answering a simple ad, with no idea what was ahead. In the following story, Steve walks us through this scenario, as well as helping us see the value in selecting young men with their hearts right (though he would never take that credit.)]

Spirit and attitude are more important than skills that can be learned.

» Steve Soderquist (1983-1985):

The Mysterious Tempo Increment

When I first came to talk to Lowell about possibly being in a Showcase band, I was perhaps twenty-one and absolutely clueless. I had answered an ad in the Tampa Tribune calling for talented musicians in the area to try out for a rock and roll band that was part of a company based out of St. Petersburg, Florida. I lived in Brandon, Florida, at the time, so was able to schedule a time to come out and speak with Lowell. He was close by with one of the bands who were staying at a hotel, scheduled to play a show nearby the next day. Upon entering the hotel, I remember walking down the hallway and some fellow with hair down his back opened his door and eyed me up and down. I nodded to him, he to me, yet not a word was spoken. Something told me he had something to do with this, however. Lowell met me in the hotel room with the band, and I soon found myself absolutely rooted to the spot by this impressively large man. He spoke with me for a few minutes, then asked me to play the guitar. His words were, "Let's see you shred."

Those who know me know that, of all the things I do musically, "shredding" is NOT one of them. I was a rhythm guitarist, with little to no knowledge of lead. Oh, I could play the solo to Boston's "More Than a Feeling," but that was the extent of my "shredding." I fumbled along, as Lowell kept encouraging me to "move around" and, I assume, present some showmanship. When I was finished, he spoke with me a bit more before inviting me to come to the day show the next day and see the band. I will never know what Lowell saw in me, to be honest. I certainly did not have even close to the abilities of these musicians; I could not move like them to save my life. I had zero confidence. The following day, I smoked a cigarette in the car with the drummer who rode over with me from the hotel, the same fellow who I first met the night before in the hall. All around, I must have made the worst impression anyone could make. Still, Mr. Lytle saw something. He spoke with me after the show, and let me know he'd like for me to take over guitar duties for the band, as their current guitarist had home issues he needed to take care of. He went on to say I would have to quit smoking. I said I would, but that was easier said than done. I will say I made every effort, but that was something I struggled with right up until six years ago. Mr. Lytle, I did quit. Thank you for being patient.

It did not work out for me, as it soon became apparent I was woefully lacking in the 'shredding' department, to say the least. I was sent back home, but received a call a few weeks later from one of the home office gentlemen asking me to come in and try out on keyboards. Now, this was something I could get behind, much more so than the guitar. I had been playing piano for years and, thankfully, I really did have a good ear and could pick up songs rather quickly. After a visit with this man, I was soon on a Greyhound bus and on my way to meet up with my next band, which included manager and front man Mark Warfel, guitarist Craig Wiggins, bassist Kevin Hart, drummer Chris Seavers, and sound engineer Chris Bouvier. After two weeks of sitting in the hotel room day and night to learn the current line-up, the other keyboardist went home, and I was on my own. Nothing about this is an easy story. I struggled through more self-doubt and fear than I would have ever cared to admit, but I think this boat was rather full. However, I received encouragement, and stuck to my guns. Soon, I stopped being so rigid, and fell into the camaraderie that only those in Young American Showcase can truly know. We were more than a band; we were family.

SHOW CAMP

*Lowell: I paid good money for those monitors;
you should USE them!*

The first step for all new band members was always show camp, a four-week, non-stop, grueling, adrenaline-pumping, limit-pushing, crowd-thinning, high-octane rush of preparation that ended with each band piling into their step vans full of equipment and luggage and heading for their first gig, some driving all night to get there.

How did prospective band members make it to show camp? Every year, all year long, audition tapes poured in and players were selected to attend show camp the following summer. Attending show camp was not a guarantee; as we have mentioned, all newbies were required to buy two plane tickets—one to Florida, and one to return home, a stark reminder their audition was not over. At the beginning, camp started out as a large group of individual musicians. For the most part, bands were not completely formed yet. The leadership team had to make many decisions in that first week on who would be the best to fill a slot in any particular group. In addition to covering instruments and front man talent, they also made efforts to include at least one veteran Showcase musician in each band to help the rookies adjust and learn the road life more quickly. Additionally, they wanted a variety of personalities, backgrounds, and personas in each band, each one designed to reach their own niche of audience members, almost like casting a play. If they were to achieve their mission of reaching **everyone**, the band members could not all look and act the same. Just like the popular group The Monkees, in each band they tried to place a comedian like Peter Tork, a tough-guy hard rocker like Micky Dolenz, a dark, shy, and brooding character like Michael Nesmith, and, of course, a "pretty boy" like Davy Jones. They also tried to make sure each group was racially mixed, like their audiences would be. The first band's experience in Port St. Joe, Florida, proved how important this would be.

Beyond this, one of the spiritual directors, Joe Lathrop, introduced the idea of using Tim LaHaye's concepts found in his book, Spirit-Controlled Temperament

(1966) to ensure the bands were balanced by spiritual temperament, as much as possible. Lowell remembers it this way:

» Lowell Lytle:

Tim LaHaye wrote a book entitled *Spirit-Controlled Temperament*, which describes four different types of human nature, or temperaments, that people have, as well as their strengths and weaknesses, and how they can be strengthened when under the control of the Holy Spirit. In order to put a successful band of musicians together we tried to find at least one of each different temperament for each band. The four temperaments were Sanguine, Choleric, Melancholic, and Phlegmatic. All four of them have good points and bad points.

The Sanguine would like to start parties. That's good. The negative side? He doesn't pay attention to details. For example, if you asked him to go paint a wall he would probably do it in an extremely short time. He would call you and say, "Look. I'm done." He no doubt would be standing there with a paintbrush in his hand, the paint dripping off onto the floor, which he never bothered to cover first.

The Choleric would be a leader. He is like a sergeant in the army. He makes things happen. That's good. The only problem is, he steps on people. That's bad.

The Melancholic would be negative. Nothing is going to work right. He brings people down. The good side of him is that he pays attention to details. He puts his shoes together at night.

The Phlegmatic would be wise, but as a rule he would be slow. However, he would get things done, no matter how long it took.

If you were going to tell a story about each one it would sound like this. The first one would say, "I got a great idea, let's go on a picnic.

The second one would say, "Okay Harley, you will leave early and go to the park and reserve the pavilion. Everyone else, we're going to leave here at 9 o'clock sharp! That's it. And we're going to HAVE A GOOD TIME!"

The third one would say, "Oh, I don't know, I think that cloud is going to turn dark and it's going to rain."

The fourth one would say, "Oh, I remember picnics when I was a kid. The potato sack race, sliding down the slide, eating watermelon. That was so much fun; but why do we have to go anywhere? Why don't we just have it here on my front porch?"

We all have some of each; some good, and some bad. Christ had all of the good and none of the bad. I remember our staff sitting around in a circle with pictures of each person, trying to figure who had what temperament. How did they look? Could they get along together? We did that into the wee hours of the morning. That was challenging, to say the least. Of course, the physical appearance and background played a role—"pretty boy," etc.—and the instruments had to be right. The key to a strong band would be balance in all those areas, especially temperament.

[Several band members have mentioned studying this book on the road. The company leadership clearly took it seriously. Over the years, other similar tools have come along, such as the Enneagram commonly used today in secular applications, but this one was the first that would include the Holy Spirit's influence on our natural strengths and weaknesses, and proved to be a powerful tool for forming bands and mentoring them on the road. Following are show camp and audition stories from throughout the Showcase experience. Connie Kolosey sets the stage for us:]

» Connie Kolosey (1970-1980):

Raised by Wolves

At the first Young American Showcase Rehearsal Camp in August of 1970, I was one month short of my fourteenth birthday. I was there for most of it as the babysitter for Lowell and Barb's children, David (10), Debbie (7), and Laura (4). The camp was held at New College in Sarasota; Lowell was putting together four bands to start touring in September. The New College campus was split by US 41 with the dorms where we stayed on the west side and the classrooms where the bands rehearsed on the east side. It was a long, hot walk across sandspur-filled fields and the busy highway to get between the two, a trek I made many times over the following years.

All of the buildings were in a modernistic modular cement design. Although they were less than ten years old at that time, they appeared not to be aging well and were already in need of an interior remodel. The carpets were musty and the fixtures were corroding. In the heat and humidity of the Florida August, the rooms always felt damp and overly air-conditioned. I have a strong image of condensation on the windows.

Being a kid, I had little understanding of what was happening from a business standpoint, and now, all these years later, I only have snippets of memories, more impressions than distinct events. My ideas of what was important centered on my interactions with the cast of characters. The guys would joke, and tease, and flirt, and I was infatuated with all of them. Most of my memories are scenes from late at night after the bands finished rehearsing for the day. One such memory was hanging out with Barb in the dorm room after the kids were asleep. She would be working on the finances, accounts payable only, I presume—there were no accounts receivable at that point. Looking back, I have no idea where the money came from or how they funded the initial operation. We chatted casually as I thumbed through a *Billboard* magazine. She suggested we play a game wherein I would read the titles of the songs listed on the top 100 charts strung together as if I were reading a story. We laughed so hard at the silliness we could not speak. For me, as an adolescent girl, this type of personal interaction with an adult woman and role model was very formative in my development.

That same year, Lowell was so excited about this guy named Lance Abair, whom they had just met. I recall seeing Lance and Linda, and little blonde-headed Mindy, from across a parking lot late one night. They looked unbearably cool; Linda with her short bleach-blonde hair and Lance with his long, bushy mane. They looked nothing like the fuddy-duddy Baptists I grew up with—which, of course, was the point. One night, Lance was performing with his band, the *Fabulous Entertainers*, at a

The Abairs at Show Camp: Lance, Linda, and Mindi
Photo courtesy of Doug Manor

bar in St. Petersburg. Understand, the Lytles were very conservative and would not normally visit "this type of establishment." However, Lowell wanted his musicians to see how the pros do it. He loaded up all the guys in various vehicles. I squeezed into the back of their big yellow Chevrolet station wagon, and off to The Lounge we all went. If anyone thought twice about having a 13-year-old girl in tow, I was not aware of it. I think probably I was along because I needed to get back home in St. Pete that night, but it was all very strange and exciting.

[You will hear directly from Lance later in the book. His story reminds us of the power of an uncompromising witness. The full story of how Lowell connected with Lance Abair is tucked in Diving into the Deep *in a chapter aptly called, "Only Lance."].*

On another night, I needed a ride from camp back to St. Petersburg. After rehearsals had stopped, a couple of the guys (one was a manager and performer named Ron McCracken, who in his late twenties seemed a lot older that the other guys) planned to drive to St. Pete to go to Michael Braun's, so they were elected to take the baby-sitter home. It was at least 11:00 p.m. and my parents' house was well

Ticket/calling card, Michael Braun's place

past Michael Braun's place, so I was with them when they stopped. Michael Braun was the go-to clothing designer for rock and roll pros. He designed for Jimmy Hendrix and dozens of other top-tier artists, and, of course, was a friend of Lowell's and happy to help style the guys in the bands. A signature piece from his collection would become a valuable collector's item, but at this point, the guys just wanted to find the right shirts and jeans to give them "that look." Michael's place was an aging white Victorian with a wrap-around porch that sat on a hill near 22nd Avenue South. At night, it looked haunted!

While the guys were in another room talking with Michael, I sat in the living room and waited. The room was large and cluttered with clothing, papers, and outdated furniture. Music was playing loudly and people were smoking. Various people would walk through the room, paying no attention to me. A very tall guy with really long blond hair, wearing tightknit Braun-style bell-bottoms and no shirt, danced through the living room a couple of times. Toni, Michael's assistant, was in one room with a guy sporting a large afro. Her hair was also wild, long, and curly, and her clothes were revealing. She appeared to be moving between helping Michael with the Showcase guys and entertaining her guest. It was all a sensory overload for a thirteen-year-old sheltered kid. I am sure it was not a scene my parents expected me to be a part of, and I doubt the Lytles knew I was there, either. Nonetheless, everyone was kind to me and I was perfectly safe.

One of the Showcase methods which some might scrutinize was the importance of presentation, of creating the illusion of fame, celebrity, and the rock and roll persona both on and off the stage, whenever the bands were in public. In reality, these bands were made up primarily of small town boys, all of whom professed Jesus as their Lord and Savior. Why the illusion? Wasn't that being deceitful?

Lowell learned early in life, through his days performing magic shows and ventriloquism, the power of illusion and misdirection. You convince the audience they are seeing one thing; when they see something else, something completely unexpected, you have their attention—and awe. Remember, the goal was to reach young people who had come to idolize the cultural kingpins of sex, drugs, and rock and roll, who may have rejected the thought that a life in Christ could be anything other than a boring, out-of-touch, hypocritical, outdated religion. How better to do that than give them what they thought they wanted? Lowell often referred to 1 Corinthians 9:19–23:

> **Though I am free and belong to no one, I have made myself a slave to everyone, to win as many as possible. To the Jews I became like a Jew, to win the Jews. To those under the law I became like one under the law (though I myself am not under the law), so as to win those under the law. To those not having the law I became like one not having the**

law (though I am not free from God's law but am under Christ's law), so as to win those not having the law. To the weak I became weak, to win the weak. I have become all things to all people so that by all possible means I might save some. I do all this for the sake of the gospel, that I may share in its blessings.

Outwardly, the band members would become all things to all people. By behavior, most remained steadfast to the tenets of their faith—and the very strict rules of the road, which we will cover later in the book. To do otherwise would mean a one-way ticket home. Guys received rocker hairstyles, and were taught how to interact with people in public so as to present themselves as confident, accepting, and always "totally pro"—skills that served them well after Showcase. Both their street clothes and performance attire made them stand out, and created a vibe students were immediately drawn to (and which, predictably, repelled conservative adults). Band members were required to provide their own clothes and few, if any, came from a wealthy background. Consequently, most scrimped and saved as much of their weekly per diem money as they could to be able to add a couple of key Michael Braun pieces to their wardrobe. You will find more on the Braun effect later in the book.

Early Free Fare muscle car with paint-matched van

The first band, you may recall, drove eye-catching sports cars with custom-painted surfboards racked to the roof. For the first few years each band had a custom-detailed muscle car with matching paint on the van. This expensive attention-getter did not last long, however; the equipment the bands used was even more important—and expensive. In the end, it mattered very little what first impression a band made, how high their energy, or how perfect their performance, *if the sound coming out of their system was not equal to the task. A few members of the management team would attend the annual NAMM Show (National Association of Music Merchants) in Chicago to see what equipment was coming out and to network. One of the bookers, Bob Miller, realized it would be a "win-win" if any of those companies were to sponsor Young American Showcase by providing their equipment for all of the bands. Showcase would get top of the line equipment, in exchange for free exposure of that equipment to well over a million students per year, and road-tested product improvement feedback. Miller put the first deal together with SUNN Amplifiers in Tualatin, Oregon, and the path was set. Lance Abair remembers going up to Chicago every year, wearing a suit with his bushy hair and chops, to network with the presidents of the equipment companies, make connections, get the deals, maintain the relationships, and arrange for Showcase bands to play the show, alongside the top players in the industry, such as Larry Londin, Elvis's drummer, and world-renowned guitarist and inventor of the first solid body electric guitar, Les Paul.*

Lance Abair, ready for NAMM

Lance employed a "make it happen" strategy to find the best companies available and convince them to sponsor the groups, providing new, top of the line, beautiful equipment such as Moog synthesizers, Korg keyboards, Epiphone and Gibson guitars and basses, drums from Yamaha, Premiere, Slingerland, and Pearl, Zildjian cymbals, Peavey everything, Lab Series amplifiers, Bi-Amp and Electro-Voice sound systems. All served the broader purpose of providing the best possible sound, the highest-level show possible in that day to help each band earn the right to be heard through their stunning performance—a brilliant strategy and a key component to the Showcase method.

Les Paul with YAS player Paul Turner at NAMM 1976

Earn the right to be heard.

The 1976 Showcase bands and equipment

[In 1976, Young American Showcase launched a group with a new angle, timed to coincide with the country's Bicentennial celebrations and give the bookers another option to try to get into new schools or bring fresh shows in to their existing schedules. The "Freedom Jam" bands came dressed in patriotic-themed costumes and delivered an extremely funny comedy show mixed with high-energy pop music in the day shows, followed by the usual high-powered Top 40 rock show in the evenings. Each night show still closed with their stand against unhealthy living and their evangelistic message.

These next stories give you a window into this group, how difficult it sometimes was to help these young men lay down their pride for the mission, and the often-unorthodox methods Lowell used to impress upon them the importance of following the script. Lowell evoked fear and trembling in the bands, particularly the rookies who had only to look up at his intense scrutinizing eyes, his 6'4" frame towering over them at camp. Lowell was the head of the company; one word from him and you were headed home. But, more than that, he was a father figure with a general's persona, someone that commanded respect and demanded compliance, but also was beloved to the veteran players. His tough demeanor during show camp was no accident—and all part of the Showcase method.

Typical Freedom jam costumes. Clockwise from top: Kenny Williamson, Bill Fairfield, Aaron Stillings, Alec Johannson, Corey Fleig, Gary Kolosey, Mark Lach (center).

Be the leader others can trust and must follow.

» John Gunden (1977-   ):

Back to the Chicken Farm

It was August 1977; I was eighteen and aimless and had only been a Christian for a year prior to my Showcase journey. I was considered "pretty cool" in my little rural high school and thought I knew a few things. I loved rock and roll like all Midwesterners, but one thing I *knew* that I knew was that Elvis Presley was not even remotely cool. *[The editors beg to differ.]*

As we were putting the Freedom Jam show together at New College, Lowell came in to check things out and announced that I would be doing the Elvis skit. I hated Elvis. I mean, I saw one of the guys do the routine and found it funny but I could not see myself doing it. I resisted Lowell Lytle, something I learned not to do. He unleashed the, "I will win and you will lose" method to the fullest!

He told me that if I wasn't ready by tomorrow I would be flying back to Michigan to go back to work on my father's chicken farm, in front of all the guys I was just learning to know. I was humiliated and angry. I wondered if he was even a Christian. It bruised my pride—and I did not want to go back home a failure.

Lowell: You've got to believe YOU'RE Elvis!

So I got a cassette of the routine and practiced late into the night, memorizing my lines and looking in the mirror, curling my lip and trying to act and sound like the dreaded Elvis! I was okay at it—but not at all sure things would work out.

The next day came, and Lowell entered the rehearsal room with twenty cheerleaders marching behind him. I still don't know the full story behind that, but I am sure Lowell was working his magic and trying to give me a vision for what it could be. The funny thing is I believed it was legit! I thought they really liked my performance! He had them screaming and going nuts!

Lowell was not finished humiliating me, I was sure of it. Later that year, he came out to Connecticut to watch and evaluate our show. I was nervous he was going to be hard on me again. After the show, we all gathered to hear his critique. He was tough on all five of the other guys, but then he came to me and his eyes lit up and he went on to give me the highest praise—a kindness that I surely did not deserve. I was embarrassed that the guys got chewed out—and I didn't. I was, in my estimation, the least talented guy in the band. Corey Fleig was the real talent, singing "Baby Come Back" and "Dream On" with such accuracy. Me? I was closer to Fred Flintstone singing "I Wanna Rock and Roll All Night."

Nevertheless, after singing the same old songs over and over, the brightest spot in the show for me was always the Elvis skit; it was just fun to make people laugh. I learned that I did not know everything I thought I knew. I respected Lowell and Lance's professional insight and the methods they taught us: Make it happen; I will win and you will lose; [boozh-boozh] Dead air! He taught us how to sell it, and it all worked.

[Leaders sometimes forget that their followers are often easily intimidated, sometimes desperate to win their approval, and willing to follow them over a cliff if necessary, trusting that their leader knows what they are talking about and always has their best interests at heart. This is not always the case, of course, and certainly

even the great Lowell Lytle made his mistakes over the years. Still, he was able to instill an unwavering loyalty to the mission in everyone that ultimately gave them the will to push past rough spots and human failings.

There is no end to the stories about rehearsal camp, but what exactly happened during those four weeks? How could you possibly throw five super-ego young guys who had never met each other into a room together for four weeks and have them come out as a "totally pro," high-octane, stunningly exhilarating rock and roll band, dressed, rehearsed, and ready for a grueling non-stop nine-month road tour? How do you get them to gel together, musically, professionally, emotionally, mentally, and spiritually? What about all the other details that would have to be covered? The next two stories give you a window into that world.]

» Michael (Jonesy) Jones (1980–1982):

Overwhelmed and Intimidated

I was introduced to Showcase without ever seeing one of the bands. My brother Gary was in a Christian band in Ft. Wayne, Indiana. They were warming up for Phil Keaggy, a nationally known Christian artist (and still one of the best guitarists in any genre). They started the show short a band member and they were okay, but after the second song, this crazy man runs up on stage to the grand piano, counts off the song, and kicked the piano bench upstage as he pounded on the keys on his feet. The "okay" band is now killing it. This keyboard player was all you could watch; he seemed to have a lot of friends in the audience. I'm a shy guy, but felt compelled to tell this guy how much I enjoyed his show. "It must have been great to play for all your friends," I told him. He looked confused and told me he didn't know anyone there. "But what about all those people you were pointing at, and laughing with?"

Marty Wright in action, Rich Thomas on bass.
Photo courtesy of Paul Turner

"Oh that's something I learned; you could learn it too." This killer keys player was Marty Wright. He told me about Showcase, and later helped my brother and me make an audition tape and vouched for us, which went a long way to getting us to show camp.

After being accepted, I began getting my affairs sorted, quit my job, started learning the camp tape songs, and bought a round-trip plane ticket to St. Pete.

THE ROAD TO SHOWCASE

This was the first time flying for both of us. We experienced a lot of "firsts" in this adventure. Upon arrival, managers greeted us and drove us to rehearsal camp in one of the Showcase equipment trucks. I sat beside this guy from Texas, Galen Beaver (a drummer), who had a suit on. "Daddy says a Texas gentleman always wears a suit when he flies," he explained.

At camp check-in, a young woman named Cathy Zeeb greeted us all by name. She had studied our photos so she would know us by sight before she met us (impressive).

[The editors love this observation, because it shows that the expectations for being "totally pro," for "making it happen" and always bringing your best to the team permeated every aspect of the company, not just the bands. Every member of the administrative army understood the mission. They were 100 percent committed to it, and to one another. Michael observed something else; he saw in those "veteran" band members a camaraderie, a genuine love for each other and joy at being reunited. Who wouldn't want to be a part of this? All of these elements, these authentic responses, made an impression on the rookies.]

Later in the orientation, Galen and I sat beside each other in a room full of rookies. All of a sudden, the vets start coming in. They look like rock stars, and they are greeting each other with hugs. Me being a football player and Galen being a Texan, we didn't know about all this hugging. But, they had been on the road together for nine months; they were as close as brothers. How else would they greet each other? But—there was something else too.

That evening was the Vet show. The Veterans divided into bands, show clothes and everything, and performed for us. They all had what Marty Wright had—that never-ending energy and showmanship. You didn't know where to look, it was so...big! I was overwhelmed and intimidated. When we went back to our rooms, I was standing out on the balcony looking into space, telling myself that there was no way I could do that. Unexpectedly, one of the veteran guitars joined me on the balcony, a player named Marty Resch. Marty was one of the stars of the evening, tall and powerful. He played his guitar like it was a weapon. He asked me how I was doing. I pretty much told him there was no way I could do what I just witnessed. He assured me I could, adding, "...if you listen to what they tell you and do what they tell you." Marty assured me, "You should have seen me when I was first here. I had your same feelings." His encouragement helped, but I still had my doubts. This was a really big first day.

» Wes Turner (1972-1973):

Hot August Nights

Early August 1972, I flew from my home in Portland, Oregon to Fort Lauderdale, Florida, readying my mind and body to report the next day to New College for the Young American Showcase (YAS) rehearsal camp. Lowell Lytle had accepted me, on the recommendation of Justin Smith, to be the manager and lead singer for a Free Fare band.

When we first arrived at camp, we met the other guys in our group, set up instruments in a room, and had a sit-down. How the heck were we going to "wow" those school kids? We had to come up with a knockout set list, not just for the initial school assembly but for a two-hour rock concert to boot. Gathering material, deciding show line-ups, who solos when and for how long, being trained by the pros on how to get out of ourselves and invest in the audience, both musically and verbally. How much humor? Can we agree on tunes? Drilled into us daily was the need to connect to the audience, so—projecting, emoting, smiling (because we were not snarling rockers) at a blank wall and kicking it up a notch whenever Lowell and/or Lance came around. There were times I am sure Lowell felt like a baby-sitter, but in the end, YAS ended up bringing out the performer in each of us.

A band at rehearsal camp coached by Lowell and Brent Woody

Have I mentioned the humidity?

What I have not mentioned is the great time of fellowship around meals, both at the school and a restaurant off campus, and getting to know the other four bands, all with varying styles. I remember being absolutely knocked out by the power and talent surrounding us.

Righteous threads and a group photo for posters were on the agenda, as camp progressed. Michael Braun, costumer of rock and roll royalty, came in and took measurements, tossing costume ideas our way. We could not wait to see what he actually made for us.

[We have mentioned Michael Braun. Earlier, Connie helped us understand the wild atmosphere in his home and design studio. Next, Wes helps us understand the brilliance behind his work and why it was so important for bands to look the part.]

Braun's Age

Pink and blue with flowers? A flowery velveteen jacket over that? Wow! Does that match? I guess Michael Braun must know what he's doing. He had dressed Sonny and Cher, Jimi Hendrix, Vanilla Fudge, and loads more, an A to Z list in the Who's Who of Rock. Who was I to question? Then I realized—it wasn't supposed to match. We weren't the Fifth Dimension or the Young Americans. This was freakin' ROCK AND ROLL!

For us Free Fare guys, the idea of customized, made-to-fit costumes and street wear was a dream come true. These were clothes that would get people talking. They said either "rock star" or "colorblind pimp," depending on who was looking. Let's face it...they were a work of art!

Michael was an innovator and duds entrepreneur from Rye, New York, that had settled in Florida after a sailboat injury a few years earlier. He started crafting pants out of surplus navy togs because, after all, they were the original bell-bottoms. Instead of the bells pooching out to the sides of the legs, he re-structured them to run front-to-back, hence covering the shoe. He put the pant seams down the front and back of the legs and that left the sides for decorative stuff—airbrush and hand-painted designs, buttons, patches, embroidery, etc. His tenacity and marketing savvy had garnered

Turner (center) with the band in their Brauns

him some big name rock world clients in the late '60s and early '70s who valued his originality and colorful threads: Aerosmith, Allman Brothers, Bon

Jovi, Chicago, Alice Cooper, Bob Dylan, Bob Seeger, Sly Stone, The Temptations, Three Dog Night, and on and on.

He came to camp early to measure us all and talk about what we wanted… or what was best for our position. Lead singer? Flashy and flamboyant—lots of look-at-me stuff. Drummer? Party on top since no one ever saw his pants much. Guitarist? Darling of the group—more flash, especially on arms. Bass? All in black with embroidery—attitude plus. And keyboards? More up on top to add flourish to arm movements.

When costume try-on day came, we were all pretty excited. I know that at least two of the guys in my group were ecstatic about their stuff. The bass player and the guitar player got just what they wanted: black bad-#%s attitude, Chris Squire-like clothes for Dan the bassist. They matched the color of his bass—I remember that being important at the time. A great dust-colored ensemble (sort of Motown meets a Spanish dancer) with a lot of red embroidery for Justin on guitar. I think our drummer Rod's shirt was bright red, and the keyboardist was in burgundy, with patches and more detail on the pants. Mine—as you may have surmised from the opening sentence—was a pink and navy blue cowboy shirt with a black velveteen jacket with roses on it, and plain black pants. I admit I was more than a little disappointed. I had chosen these black and maroon granny shoes, and the whole outfit was a lot more flowery than what even my granny would wear. I got over it. Michael convinced me that it was a solid package.

In the early '80s, Michael was still doing rock and roll clothes, but the '80s style was more big hair, skinny ties, pegged pants, etc. Then Michael ran the "Grunge" look gauntlet: ripped T-shirts or ugly drab shirts with boxy dark-colored suit jackets hanging over ripped and dragging-the-ground jeans. He then pivoted to design neon-colored wrestling togs for WWF guys Randy "Macho Man" Savage, Tampa native Hulk Hogan, and others.

Flash forward to 2005. The *Tampa Bay Times*[1] reports that his computer-generated modern art designs are featured at the Lyssa Morgan Gallery in Tampa and the Digital Halls of Fame in Japan, England, and Sweden. Also, his custom-made Jimi Hendrix jacket hangs in the Rock & Roll Hall of Fame in Cleveland, Ohio. Wow! As I write this, there is an exhibition (costumes and a film) being mounted by a person on the West Coast interested in preserving Michael's rock and roll history.[2] We always knew he was a genius; we did not need to see his official bio to realize that, but it's great to see the entertainment and art world recognizing the brilliance. Pink and blue cowboy shirt with flowers and a flowered velveteen jacket? Did I say brilliance?

---

[1] Dave Scheiber, "Outrageousness tailor-made," Tampa Bay Tribune, September 30, 2005
[2] "Made As Art: The Michael Braun Story" on Netflix

PART THREE

THE SHOWCASE WAY

Lowell: I'm tired of being right.

Young American Showcase experimented with a few different flavors of bands, song selections, skits, and many other variables over the years, always trying to adjust the shows to the changing student culture, doing everything they could, every year, to keep the shows fresh and on point. The foundational concepts, methods, and rules, though, were not changed, or were only slightly modified if the leaders agreed upon a more effective approach. Every member internalized those golden tenets, many writing about how those basics affected them personally, professionally, and spiritually, long after their tours with Showcase were in the rear view-mirror. This set of stories illuminates many of them.

James Whitfield and Marty Resch ramp up the students at a day show.

LOVE AND ENERGY

Lowell: You guys are like death on a cracker.

As we have mentioned before, a core belief was that every band had to "earn the right to be heard." Simply put, if you do not earn the right to be heard, you won't be. All of your hard work, perhaps your only opportunity to reach any particular student, will be wasted. How do you earn the right to be heard? Love and energy.

"Love and energy" became a mantra for many groups before going onstage, and was the method they used to "earn the right to be heard." It was not enough to give an excellent performance. They had to go so far over the top that the audience felt their passion, their enthusiasm, their heart. Every word, every time they caught someone's eye or accepted their applause, every ounce of body language on and off stage, how they addressed their fans after the show, how they treated each other, had to be genuine, had to reflect their "utmost for God's highest," had to leave it all on the floor. They literally emptied themselves every single show, then packed up, moved down the road, set up, and did it all again, at a dizzying, exhausting pace. When asked what "love and energy" meant, Showcase family members share the following:

1) The giving of everything you have to the audience with unceasing effort. If your clothes are not dripping wet by the end of the second song you are not working hard enough.

2) Communicating positivity—sharing your blessings, your spiritual power, and your joy. It's what we contribute to this life that matters.

3) Because you are experiencing extreme happiness throughout the entire show, you automatically communicate that to the audience.

4) "Love and energy" was a mantra we used to chant as we were running out on stage before each show. It starts from having an honest love of people that the audience can feel by looking at your expressions—smiling, excitement, and genuine interest.

5) Right before we went on stage, our manager would remind us to project "love and energy" from the moment we ran on stage until the doors to the truck were closed and we were off the property.

[*As glamorous as being on tour felt, the students had to feel as if it was all about them, a gift, not a self-aggrandizing ego boost for the band. When you are barely out of high school yourself, this is sometimes a hard lesson to learn, as TJ explains in this next story.]*

» TJ Klay (1977–1979):
If everyone who came through Showcase was totally honest, I am sure they would admit to going through periods where they were just out there kind of playing rock star. As a Christian I wanted to tell people about Jesus, but knew this was a special kind of ministry; in Lowell's words, "you win the right to be heard," and have a special way of taking the gospel into the schools. I can only speak for myself, but I know I became caught up in "playing rock star" a time or two. I specifically remember feeling like we (I) were spinning our wheels out there a bit and that everything wasn't so spiritual, and so I prayed and asked the Lord to bring me opportunities to share. Over the next few months, I was able to pray with twelve or thirteen kids after our evening shows...WOW!

And, when you have to rotate and take turns giving the "evening rap," you get better at it, just like you get better at taking your solos or—as a bass player—playing with the drummer.

» Buddy Waterman returns:
[Buddy was part of the very first group with Lowell and Gary, until the time came for him to serve in the air force. The military lottery began December 1969, a new process that drew 19- to 25-year-olds first. Previously, men 26 and older were first to be drafted. Buddy's number was drawn three months later, while he was touring with the group. He chose instead to enlist in the air force. The Vietnam lottery ended three years later, and in 1973, Buddy's enlistment was up.]

After finishing tech school, I was assigned to Plattsburgh Air Force Base as an aircraft mechanic, until I was honorably discharged in 1973. I spent all my spare time in the air force practicing and playing guitar and drums. Plattsburgh was also a college town, so there were plenty of opportunities to play music on the weekends. Because I was not deeply rooted and grounded in God's Word and did not have any real Christian friends during those years, I was slowly backsliding. This is why it is so important to be actively part of a church family, as Hebrews 10:23–25 says:

> "Let us hold unswervingly to the hope we profess, for he who promised is faithful. And let us consider how we may spur one another on toward love and good deeds, not giving up meeting together, as some are in the habit of doing, but encouraging one another—and all the more as you see the Day approaching." (NIV)

But, God was faithful and did not leave me. In early July 1973, I received a phone call from that deep, familiar voice. Lowell informed me that they needed a musician who could play drums and guitar, and I was brought to his remembrance.

God had blessed the original rock and roll vision, and by now, Young American Showcase was preparing for their fifth school year tour. Only now, there would be five rock bands going into junior and senior high schools throughout the whole United States.

YAS was now fully staffed with a home office, band managers, bookers, backers, and Sunn Music Company as an active sponsor. Each band was driving a customized GMC step van and given a clothing allowance for "Michael and Tony's" custom show clothes.

Every second of our forty-minute assembly show was action-packed and precision-planned with a strategic dialogue that moved the crowd: from frenzy to exhilaration, from laughter to tears of joy. In hilarious skits, we would use the principal or a popular teacher as the target for embarrassment. It was all good, clean fun!

We had one goal: to get every student to our night show in order to share the most important opportunity of their lives: to receive God's greatest gift...His Son, Jesus Christ!

» Ron Lentini (1970-1985):

It was really my second time in Texas around 1974 or '75 that I became fully convinced that our concept of reaching kids with the gospel really worked. As manager, I was the only familiar face in the group for kids who had seen the show our first time through the year before. I was totally amazed and unprepared for the number of kids who would come up to me and ask what happened to Larry, and Wayne, and Rich, and Jim—the first group. They told me how much we had positively affected their school—and them. This happened literally every day that we played a school we had been to before. Hearing these kids tell me how much our closing raps meant to them and how it helped change the direction of some of their lives was why we joined Showcase. I know there will be people in Heaven because of this work and the contribution of everyone who has had a part in Young American Showcase. Our time here was the most uniquely enjoyable time in our lives. None of our current circle of friends can begin to understand what spending fourteen years with this organization has done for or meant to us. God has used it to shape us into the people we are today. For that, we are most thankful.

[Ron went from being a band manager to a booker, building relationships with principals around the country in order to get YAS in front of as many students as *possible. This next story reveals both what can happen when you find innovative ways to "earn the right to be heard," and what it looks like when you pour "love and energy" into the relationships you build, as Ron did.]*

»Tom Miller (1975–1985):

Four Freshmen

This story is about earning the right to be heard, but in a different setting. Larry Butler, Ron Lentini, and I were the bookers for Showcase at the time, and we joined Lowell Lytle at the national principals' convention in Orlando, Florida, to network and hopefully book gigs. We got there the night before and set up the booth, and Lowell thought we needed to do something to attract people's attention. "Why don't we practice the Four Freshmen, all of us, and then we will sing it the next morning to get some people around us so we can hand out literature."

So, we practiced in the cement stairwell the night before. The song was "In This Whole Wide World" and our rendition was fairly believable. The next day before we started singing, Lowell said, "We need to get a brochure in everyone's hand." When Lowell says "everyone's hand," he means it! Here we were with our brand-new Freedom Jam/Free Fare brochures. We were out of them by noon, and he was so happy that it was working so well.

Larry went for a coffee break and when he came back, he had a whole handful of brochures that he picked up in a wastebasket around the corner. We went around to all the wastebaskets and picked up all the brochures we could find, cleaned them up, and continued handing them out.

We would start singing again over the next hour or two. We would hear principals in the crowd shout out, "Ron Lentini!" That was amazing. At least thirty or forty principals remembered Ron from his previous contact with them. He would take the time necessary to talk to each of them. We would sing the Four Freshmen number, and people would just gather around. After a while, we noticed people were spending more time in the booth next to ours. It had sports paraphernalia, and the man who owned the booth was juggling three beanbags that he had made and was selling. People were not watching us—they were watching him.

Mid-afternoon, Lowell came back to the booth, juggling. "I got a set of these from the guy next door," he said.

I asked, "Did you bring us any?"

He replied, "I bought him out!" Problem solved. We continued our singing. I still have a set of those juggling bags.

MAKE IT HAPPEN

Lowell: I'd like a BLT.
Waitress: I'm sorry; we don't have BLTs on the menu.
Lowell: Do you have bread? Do you have bacon?
Do you have lettuce? Do you have tomatoes?
Waitress: Yes.
Lowell: Put it on a plate and bring it to me.

"Make it happen" is so baked in to the fabric of every Showcase member that, to this day, this is the phrase that everyone first references when talking about the basic concepts of Showcase. "Make it happen" is far more than "no excuses—get it done," as these stories will illustrate. They also show the complexities of road tours, and how very often those "make it happen" moments had something to do with a vehicle.

» Bobby Flake (1986-1987):

When you are on the road, everyone in the band has a job to do. My job at the time was truck maintenance. Most of the time, truck maintenance is an easy job; however, on one particular night in British Columbia, after a show and between cities, truck maintenance became a little more exciting. We were driving late at night, and I was navigating. My eyes were bouncing between reading the map and watching the road go by. While studying the map, I saw a flash out of the corner of my eye. Something had shot past the truck and into the woods beside the highway. Before my mind had a chance to process what had just happened, the truck suddenly moved in a way that was completely unnatural as an awful, grinding sound filled the air and sparks lit up my rearview mirror. The truck came to a rapid stop and we all got out to see what had just happened. We stood there in disbelief. For a moment, we were speechless. There was a substantial groove carved into the highway that led to the melted, smoldering pavement surrounding what was left of our axle. After a long silence, someone looked at me and said, "Truck maintenance, make it happen!" Everyone except Dave and I climbed back into the Iveco and went back to sleep. We started walking down a dark Canadian highway, in the middle of the night, in search of a phone booth—the reality of "Make it happen" churning our stomachs. We had recently had some tire work done on the Iveco, and it seemed they had not put the lug nuts on properly. The flash I saw moments before was the back passenger-side tire shooting off in to the woods. The grinding sound and sparks were the axle digging into the pavement.

[Bobby brings up an interesting, common sense "make it happen" strategy. Everyone has a job to do and there are no excuses for not getting it done. Some of the guys weighed in on this important part of the Showcase design:]

» Gary Kolosey (1975-1980):

In addition to taking care of our own equipment, depending on what we played in the band, we all had other jobs to make the show happen smoothly and consistently. These other duties changed, depending on personnel and abilities. From prop manager to the PA sound system, everyone, including the manager, had additional duties to make efficient use of the limited time we had to set up, play the show, tear down, and get to the next show. Some jobs involved equipment maintenance and others were set up/tear down of all the pieces of the show. Many jobs were organizational and did not involve equipment, like dealing with the stage crew, talking to the principal, determining wake-up times and navigation. There were a lot of moving parts to the machine and it's a wonder we didn't have more problems than we did. It was mostly left up to the ingenuity and resources of the individual members of the group to "make it happen."

» Rodd Wilson (1981-1982):

To me, the most life-saving job was the stage crew guy. There was very specific training these Showcasers went through for this job. I was never in this role but certainly saw the value in it. As we all know, there were no roadies in Showcase and, without the aid of a properly motivated/coached group of students, I do not think this program would have flown. So many of our days started at 5 a.m. and ended at 11 p.m., a grueling schedule. Watching the science of the stage crew guy coach these volunteers to do the back-breaking work of unloading and positioning all the equipment and then reloading it back in (and needing it to go in a certain order or it wouldn't fit) took SO much of the burden off the band members!

Other jobs reported by the guys included:

- Find three separate 20-amp circuits to power the show. Rodd Wilson points out that failure to do so could cause an unplanned drum solo in the dark.

> *Bret Pemelton commented his manager told him he was perfect for the amp location job because he "worried like an old lady."*
- *The electrical guy also had to fix mics and amp cords that had shorted out. Mike Yocum lamented, "...sometimes REALLY late at night after a REALLY long day!"*
- *Merchandise table and inventory (posters, mostly)*
- *The back line—PA system, backdrops, drum risers, backline instruments, curtains, and song lists*
- *"Point" man—to point to the spot the volunteer roadies were to place incoming equipment*
- *Main driver*
- *Navigator and keeping the driver awake*
- *Keeping the truck cab clean*
- *Truck maintenance/truck warm-up*
- *Speaking to the music classes*
- *Wardrobe case—just kidding, no one ever did this. John Gunden commented the case was so bad costumes should have been burned by the end of tour, they stank so badly.*

» Steve Soderquist (1983-1985):

The Great Canadian Experience

Of all the things that are memorable about my time with Young American Showcase, I would be hard pressed to be able to top the experience my bandmates and I had while in Canada. Here's an abridged version.

This would have happened in the mid- '80s; the band was The Edge. This little band of merry music makers consisted of myself, keyboards and manager; Craig Wiggins, music director and guitar; John Massey, bass; Joe Theille, lead vocals; Dirk Parsons, guitar; and our sound engineer, Roddy Fischer.

I don't remember all the specifics, age and time doing their work on me, but I certainly remember the outline and then some. In a nutshell, our Iveco broke down. Kaput. DOA. And, we were told it was going to be in the shop for about two weeks, with a packed schedule ahead of us and no way to make those shows.

Ouch, right?

Now, when I called home office and started to lament our situation, it did not take long before Lowell was on the phone with me. You can imagine exactly how this call went:

Me: "Mr. Lytle, our bus is broken and we can't get to the shows. We have one scheduled for today, and our roster full of shows for the whole time the mechanic told me our ship is going to be docked. I'm not sure what you want me to do about it, but I'm thinking we need to cancel and reschedule."

Lowell Lytle: [Silence]

Me: "I know it's going to take time, but even if the shows have to be scheduled next year, that's better than nothing."

Lowell Lytle: [Silence]

Me: (coughs nervously) "So, anyway, that's where it's at. I'll call back when we're back on the road."

Lowell Lytle: "Steve?"

Me: "Yes, sir?"

Lowell Lytle: "Find another way, get your team, and play those schools. Make it happen."

<CLICK>

I think I stood holding the phone and staring stupidly at it for about three minutes. Make it happen? How? Where do I start? Can we strap our gear on our backs and walk?

No…he meant, have faith, leave God's business to God, and act on that faith.

I made some calls, and soon we had a U-Haul rented for the equipment. Looking at the local paper, I saw an ad for cars for sale, and this one gentleman had about ten. I called him and explained who I was, what YAS was, what our mission was, and he agreed to let us rent a beat-up old station wagon from the '70s until the Iveco was fixed.

This is how we made it happen. It was crazy; it was amazing! And, nothing beats the look on the kids' faces at a school we were playing when a National Lampoon station wagon followed by a twenty-foot U-Haul pulled up and a bunch of longhaired, Spandex-wearing rockers stepped out. We had made it happen.

Soon enough, our Iveco was fixed and we were on our way.

"Make it happen" is not just three words put together—it's a prayer. It's faith. Making it happen is stepping off the cliff and trusting God will place stones under your feet. We are called to continue the work of the Father, not on our time, but His, even if it takes a station wagon, a U-Haul, and what turned out to be one of the best and most memorable times in our lives.

Thanks, Lowell. Your lessons still resonate with me.

TOTALLY PRO

Lance: If you do die on stage tonight, it won't be the last time.

Several members have already mentioned one of the underlying tenets of Showcase performance: "Totally Pro." Band members, managers, anyone who was public facing, were taught to pay attention to every detail, so that in all ways, at all times, they were projecting an image that would draw the audience in, attract them, and in every detail, help the band "earn the right to be heard." This followed Lowell's understanding of the apostle Paul's methods expressed in I Corinthians 9:22, becoming "all things to all people so that by all possible means I might save some."

Clark Nauert "leaving it all on the floor."
Photo courtesy of Paul Turner

In addition to absolute professionalism and maintaining their physical appearance to fit the role they were playing, they were taught performance skills like the applause cycle, the all-important art of smiling, making eye contact, leaving it all on the floor, breaking the audience up into sections, acting the way they wanted to be perceived, and everyone went through Lance's unique class on respecting the audience.

» Lance Abair (1972-1983):

"Gracefully receiving applause" training

Since everything on stage must be real and not faked, we had a ritual at camp to teach how a performer should receive applause. We all sat in a room filled with all the Showcasers, minus the new rookies, who were instructed to wait backstage until their turn to come onstage and receive applause "with sincerity."

All members of the audience brought several pairs of rolled-up socks.

One by one, the rookies would walk out onto the stage to the applause from the audience. The rookie would either show genuine sincerity as he was thanking the audience or come across as phony.

At the first sight of a phony response, the audience would immediately pelt the rookie with all the rolled up socks, and we would instruct the rookie to go backstage and try it again. He would do this as many times as it took until he could gather up enough vulnerability to thank them graciously for their applause.

Audiences can recognize, and respond to, sincerity.

ROAD RULES

Lowell: How about if your life depended on it? Could you do it then?

The company had some very strict rules of behavior. Disobeying them might result in a special visit from home office, which in turn could lead to a one-way ticket home. Each band had a manager; sometimes the manager was also a performer. The manager was responsible for interacting with the principal and other staff members on arrival. He delegated responsibilities and supervised all of the work that had to be done before and after each show and on the road, handling unexpected events, and often running sound during the show. He kept the guys on track and on time, and helped maintain the health and safety of the band members while they were on the road. The manager had to juggle being "the boss" with mentoring the band members, caring for their mental, physical, and spiritual health, and building lifelong friendships with them. He looked out for the band, but also had to keep himself in the right frame of mind at all times. Some managers traveled with their wives, and you will hear from Connie later about what this dynamic was like.

Managers were responsible for holding band members accountable, with varied levels of success. Spiritually, many bands had daily devotions together. Bands would circle up in the school's locker room before their show to pray together. Then, of course, there were those hours, days, weeks, months on the road together, five or six guys crammed into the front of a retrofitted cargo van with a couple of sleeping berths, chairs, and lots of fast-food containers. After the excitement and novelty wore off, this was where the real test of each other's patience, commitment, and character happened. Inside the obviously challenging close quarters, true growth and bonding took place—as well as a good bit of conflict, as young bucks had to realize they didn't need to fight or jockey for power in the group. Instead, they had to learn to work as a team—more than a team, a single unit. Their mission, their witness, their success, depended on it. To do that, they needed rules. For example, in no particular order:

Rule #1: No smoking or drinking on the road. *("No drugs" was assumed.) No one on the road was allowed to smoke or drink, and of course, there was no tolerance of marijuana or drug use. Smoking might have received some latitude while members tried to quit, or a glass of wine or beer might be allowed for special dinners, but not when students were present. Drug use would send you packing immediately. Band members' actions spoke much louder than their words, and the culture of "sex, drugs, and rock and roll" were exactly what these groups were charged with countering. Their entire message would be compromised, and their witness, if they said one thing but did another. This also applied to the next rule, which was harder to manage.*

Mike Yokum mobbed at the merchandise table

Rule #2: No fraternizing with students. *When bands ran out onto the stage and began performing, students were experiencing something most had never seen before: an up-close seat to a performance on par with everything they imagined a rock icon's concert would be. The music was powerful, excellently performed, all pro, and very loud, bass and drums pounding in their chests. And the guys! Connie already described what it felt like to be around them. Just like Connie, the girls* were instantly smitten and the guys just wanted to be them, as Dave Walker's story described. The students were screaming, stomping, clapping, and cheering at every turn. Each student subconsciously picked their favorite. They had rocker hairstyles, outrageous costumes, and they looked right at you and smiled as if they were singing directly to you—and they were—just as they had been trained to do. After the concert, they stayed as long as necessary to greet students, sign autographs, sell and sign their face posters, which also gave them time to follow up with students wanting to talk about God, or about joining YAS after high school. This up-close contact with students sometimes just a year or so younger who were already enamored by them created an environment with great potential for harm.

No dating, no physical relationship, however innocuous, was allowed between band members and the students. None. Not only were the students vulnerable, so were the guys. Take a group of handsome, talented, highly personable and energetic young men dressed as rockers, doing everything they can to win the audience's undying affection, men who are apart from any girlfriends they may have for months at a time or who are completely unattached, and put them in front of several hundred impressionable female teens every day literally screaming their adoration and melting at the chance to get close to them. You are going to see sparks fly, phone numbers and addresses shared, and hearts broken. Guys were permitted to have long-distance contact, but striking up a romantic relationship with a student was not only unlawful but also definitely unprofitable, and could result in the band member being sent home immediately. This was a hard rule to follow, and some managers may or may not have applied some grace in their enforcement. However, for a few band members, this was an impossible ask. The editors are glad that one band member shared the following story from his perspective at the time, a description that perfectly illustrates the issue. Hiroshi Upshur was in YAS for a number of years, wowing audiences as an extremely dynamic, talented, and charismatic front man. He went on to enjoy an impressive career in entertainment, as did many others, but at the time, he was just one of the guys in an amazing band. In the following case, the manager saw that his band members were crossing the line.

» Hiroshi Upshur (1970-1975):

I thought I was in love

Phil Hardley, one of my later managers, called a group meeting and, acting like a tough manager, told us there would be no dating the girls from the high schools, and we agreed. He made his point. Company policy. Still, on a night off, the whole group of guys all had "dates" we arranged to meet at a movie theater in a nearby mall. Who walked in? You guessed it—Phil. Where in the Bible does it say a musician can't date a high school girl where he played? Who knows, I may meet my future ex-wife!

Hiroshi's attitude was rebellious and unflinching and the other band members followed his lead, which most definitely affected their mission. Later, Hiroshi would admit that his focus during those years was "all about me." He recognized he had a lot to learn. Ultimately, Lowell and others had to come in to help; changes had to be made—a tough and painful situation for everyone, and not unique to this particular band. In fact, Hiroshi almost did meet his "future ex-wife" on that tour. So, what about all of the young women that band members met who were already Christ-followers? Wasn't this a great way to meet strong Christian women you would never have met otherwise?

One reason why dating students was not allowed? Young men exposed to the rush of being on stage and being adored by so many young women had a hard time processing their feelings rationally—and so did the young women. Secondly and more to the point, fraternizing with minors was a recipe for disaster, and doing so immediately took the focus off of their mission of sharing their faith. It also set the band, and the company, up for a fall of gigantic proportions that could have kept untold numbers of young people from being reached with the gospel. It is a testament to leadership's determination to handle situations like this with a firm, loving, Christlike hand that no such disaster ever happened throughout the twenty-two-year history of Showcase. And many a young man learned something about relationships, and themselves—sometimes the hard way. Hiroshi's next story illustrates:]

In one city, I met a beautiful high school girl and I thought I was in love. We found ways to keep our relationship going, even though there was no dating allowed. She introduced me to her parents. I visited the family over Thanksgiving and Christmas, and actually proposed. We planned to get married the summer after she graduated from high school. In Free Fare, we would go from one city to the next. We ended up in San Antonio, Texas, where I met another young woman and thought I loved her too. I had to face the truth. I was not ready for marriage. After that, I had friendships with many women. At least ten times, I met women that, in my mind, I could have married. Now, the purpose of sharing this is to demonstrate my lack of understanding in the relationship department at that age, in that environment. It took me years to realize that attraction does not mean love. I thought being very much attracted to a woman meant I loved her. I would get these feelings of missing her, and the mind is so great for finding my car keys, but not so much in life's issues.

[Later on, you will read about other things Hiroshi learned during his YAS experience. Showcase veterans mentioned the example, and the standard, Lowell set for relationships that went beyond company rules. This standard illustrates the importance Lowell and his wife Barb, the managers, trainers, even returning musicians saw in pouring themselves into these young Showcase men and women, mentoring them, helping them mature and make the best possible life choices in all areas, not just matters of the heart. Many young men coming in to the program previously never had an older male role model talk to them about relationships, marriage, finding and caring for your life partner, and respecting women. Many did not have a role model for working hard, expecting more from yourself, growing spiritually, living a life of integrity and honor. Being thrust into this adrenaline-charged, extremely demanding and confusing environment required personal strength and maturity beyond their years, which in turn required most of these young people to grow up—quickly. To do that, they needed more than a boss, more than a manager, more than a set of rules, standards, and expectations. They needed mentors to come alongside them. Almost every veteran spoke about this aspect of his experience with deep gratitude.]

Rule #3: No female band members. *In the same vein, all of the groups were guys-only. Not only did this save money and simplify rooming and pre-show arrangements, but also it helped ensure that observant students, parents, school staff, and the public would not make assumptions about sexual promiscuity within the band, something that would instantly kill the integrity that allowed them to "earn the right to be heard." Certainly, this would be a difficult rule to keep today, in an era when women can and should no longer be excluded or held back from opportunity because of their gender, a particularly prevalent issue in Christian ministry still. Other solutions could be found today to address the very real and competing issues of gifted women being denied leadership roles in such a ministry, and the critical need to maintain an environment that is beyond reproach, with transparency and accountability in the public eye. Looking back, one can easily see that having female musicians in the band would have had a tremendous impact, but then, in the '70s, '80s, and '90s, it was a non-starter. Married managers were permitted to bring along their wives on tour. When wives were on the road, those bands benefited greatly from having their perspective, help, encouragement, and watchful attention. Some might look back on women's roles in Showcase as subordinate. However, everyone knew that Showcase could not have succeeded without the critical work done at home office, primarily by women. Lowell's wife, Barb, was an essential partner in the ministry, as everyone recognized.*

THE WOMEN OF SHOWCASE

The home office staff members, most of whom were women, played an invaluable role. Under Barb Lytle's management, they administered the affairs of what had become a very large and challenging undertaking. There were four to eight women working in the office at the peak. Most years, two or three women were on the road with their manager/spouses, and at several

Terri (Hansen) Sarchione, Valorie McNabb Pope, Cathy (Zeeb) Golladay, Sue Busch, Debbie Lytle, Jackie Thayer

points, one woman worked on the road as a booker, whom we will hear from later. Lowell's wife, Barb, took care of the books, managed the office staff, advised her husband, and ran the administrative side of the company. She also trained the managers on how to handle the sales and receipts every year and kept them in line. However, she was far more than an astute businessperson, mom, and wife.

Barb passed away in 2014. Her influence certainly shaped Lowell's decisions, her partnership brought balance, but her Showcase family most remembered her for the love.

> **Pay attention to your team. Mentor them. Show them you care.**

Barb took as much care with mentoring her staff as managers did on the road with band members. In addition, musicians saw her as their surrogate mom while they were away from home. Members describe her as "phenomenal, amazing, precious, patient," and more—all the characteristics we look for in our mom, and wish for in our boss. Her presence at show camp was a huge balancing factor, and her leadership in the company was an extension of the mission, and critical to its success. Wives, staff, and musicians weigh in:

Carren Arthur: She made me feel like I belonged, even if it was just to her.

Lang Bliss: I remember that she taught me how to balance my checking account. I felt totally accepted and understood by her. She was patient and encouraging; she was like a mom to me in ways I had not experienced with my own mom.

Rosco Cooper: I learned how to hang on to receipts because of Barb. When they pile up today, I think of her often.

Peter Eldred: She could turn one dollar into two.

Ellen Lain: She would take us out to breakfast individually, just to get to know us and support us.

Michael Hunt: She treated everyone with equal importance; no judgment in her eyes, only compassion.

Mary Beth Cosentino: She inspired me to be a godly woman. She never gave up on me when I failed and cheered me on when I succeeded.

Tom Krause: She was mom to many kids who had never been away from home much.

John Gunden: Lowell wanted to send me home but Barb felt sorry for me. *[The editors wonder how many band members were kept because Barb saw something in them.]*

Hiroshi Upshur: A beautiful woman who was always kind and loving to me. Lowell wore the pants; Barb wore the suspenders.

[Vicky Turnage was one of those students who met Christ through a Showcase concert. Soon after, she found herself working for Showcase and growing quickly in her new life in Christ under Barb's training and mentoring.]

»Vicky (Best) Turnage (1970-1985):

I met Free Fare for the first time at St. Pete High. Our group of friends had lost a friend recently due to recklessness with a rifle. A few young men were fooling around and pointing it irresponsibly at each other, someone knocked the rifle away, and it spun around and hit our friend, Tom, killing him instantly. He was only seventeen. My first close-up experience with death started me on my spiritual path, and a couple weeks later Free Fare came to our school. My friend Cindy attended St. Pete High at the time and said it might lift our spirits up to attend the evening concert. And it did! However, it was not until Gary Horton came a few days later to a group meeting I had attended and answered our many questions that I accepted Yeshua into my life. Because I did not grow up in a traditional church-going family, the whole concept of the Bible was new to me.

Barb and Lowell were willing to take the time to explain, provide materials, and answer my many questions as my spiritual journey began.

We had fun going to the different shows in the state and the guys were always respectful and kind to us. We were welcomed to the Lytle home many times, and Barb and I hit it off. She knew I was taking a typing class at school (yes, that's what it was called!), and I had just gotten my driver's license, so she offered me a part-time job to type envelopes to send follow-up materials to those kids interested in learning more about their faith. I had to read all the scribbles on the back of the tickets to decipher names and addresses, and use a huge book to locate zip codes (there was no internet or searching with Google at the time). When I graduated from school, Barb and Lowell offered me a full-time job to learn bookkeeping for the company, and I continued to be their bookkeeper for the next thirteen years! There were many changes in business practices during that time so the bookkeeping job was always a learning experience.

Barb *was my mentor. She listened and spoke carefully when teaching me about work, faith, and life. I never felt her judge; she encouraged you to think and figure it out yourself.*

[With their regular contact with various members of the groups, it is no surprise that many of the women of Showcase met and eventually married their life partners through their work with Young American Showcase. Connie Kolosey, who literally grew up in Showcase, found her match in a captivating Massachusetts guitar hero named Gary. Wives on the road had a unique perspective and role. Connie's recollections of life on the road give a wonderful picture of the bonds that formed on the road, and what life was like away from home for so long. She also gives a great snapshot of a typical weekly schedule—punishing, to say the least.]

» Connie Kolosey (1970–1980):

Married, with children

Lowell used to say, "Connie, I spend thousands of dollars in order for you to find your right man." Certainly, it was a lot of fun to be one of a few single women working for a company that brought in young musicians from all over the United States. I dated very few guys who were not Showcase guys. To me, the high school boys could not have been more mundane when compared to the Showcase musicians. In late 1974, a guy from Massachusetts named Gary Kolosey called the Showcase office. He was funny and flirty and before we hung up, he asked me what kind of wedding I wanted. He ended up joining a band that was put together in January of 1975. Initially, he appeared to me to be just one of the many cool guys to come through, but over time, we got to know each other, and a bond grew. We got married July 1978. Our groomsmen were fellow

Showcase musicians and managers, along with Gary's brother. Over forty years later, we are enjoying a happy life together. And so, it seems Lowell's investment paid off. Our first Showcase assignment as a married couple was managing a group that would start their tour in Tennessee.

We packed up our wedding gifts in a storage shed and in August of 1978 we reported to New College for YAS rehearsal camp, this time Gary working as a band manager. This was my eighth YAS camp. For years, the end of August had signaled the end of a flurry of activity preparing the bands to get ready for their tours. Inevitably, for me this was a sad time, but this year was different. I was finally going out too! I was able to experience the excitement and drama of the forming of the bands from a more personal perspective. The YAS leadership team would determine the people Gary and I would spend our first year of marriage with. In that choice, we were blessed! Our band was Brooke Hopkins on keyboards, John Phillips on guitar, Billy Dillon on drums, Dave Wagner on bass, and Mike Loredo as front man. These guys were so much fun and so sweet. We weren't the most successful band financially, but we were a tight family who sincerely enjoyed each other's company. Brooke had a goofy slapstick sense of humor and loved puns. Mike was a bit sarcastic with a good sense of comedic timing, Dave just enjoyed life, and John had an infectious belly laugh that made us all happy just to hear it. At mid-year, Mike left us for another band and Lee Murkey joined us as lead singer. Lee added a completely new flare to our performances and fit in well with the camaraderie of the band. The guys were motivated spiritually, and all wanted to learn and grow in faith and as musicians and performers. I believe that year was Showcase in its best-case scenario.

Connie (Watkins) and Gary Kolosey on tour

The tour started in Bristol, Tennessee. Our drives to the schools took us through the Smokey Mountains in time for the fall color. It all seemed magical. Typical of Showcase booking schedules, we usually played one or two assemblies first thing in the morning at the high school, tore down the set, hopefullygrabbed a quick lunch, and drove over to the middle school to set up for one or two assemblies there. We again tore down the set and traveled to the neighboring town we had played the day before and set up for the night show. If we were lucky, we might get a chance to stop by the hotel to rest, but usually not. Our bookers (Ron Kennedy that year and Larry Butler the following year) were seasoned Showcase schedulers and they packed the shows in like clockwork. The goal was to have a night show six nights per week with enough assemblies during the day to ensure a packed house at night. After every show, the truck got packed tightly, like a jig saw puzzle. We had student volunteers help us load and unload, but the musicians themselves had to hoist the heavy gear into the truck. Sometimes, we would be able to stay at one hotel for a week, on occasion even a month, but often, we would move every one or two nights. It was a grueling schedule and there was no opportunity for anyone to be ill or otherwise off their game in any way. When the guys hit the stage, they were expected to be "totally pro," all smiles and one-to-one eye contact with members of the audience.

[Connie's description of a typical week was the same for all of the groups. Bands typically played a dozen shows or more per week with driving in-between. This kind of schedule required a well-oiled machine, and would not have been possible without that carefully executed jigsaw puzzle truck load-in Connie mentioned.

Each school's contract required they provide about ten strong students to help move equipment; one person in each band was responsible for super-vising those kids and their own band members. This diagram shows what one of those guys drew to ensure he got it right every time; anything less and they wouldn't get everything in, and would not make their next gig on time. Learning how to pack

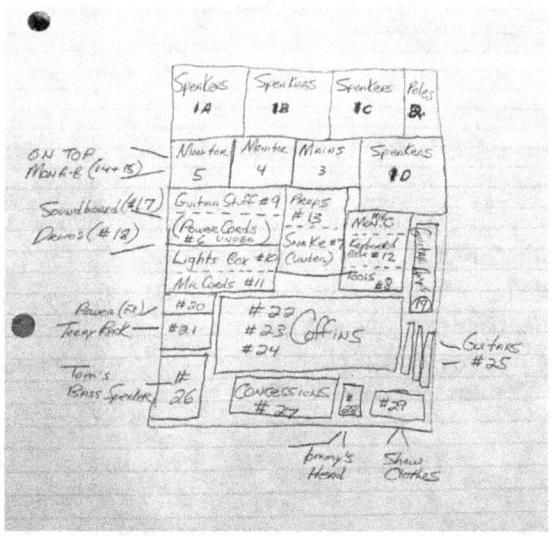

Truck loading schematic, courtesy of Jeff Siebert

the truck was the last thing each band learned at rehearsal camp before hitting the road.]

» Paul Turner (1976-1978):

The last week of camp all the bands performed four or five of their best songs for each other. Every band tried to outperform the one before, and it was great to see all the other bands. On the last night of the last week, we watched the final bands and celebrated what had been a grueling month. However, we were not done with rehearsal camp yet. After the concert, every band packed up their gear in their cases and hauled them to their truck. Bil Curry, a veteran band member in our band, supervised as we loaded our truck, a step van that had space up front just big enough for all of us. Thank God for the veteran players—we would have been all night trying to make everything fit! By the time we finished, it was late at night and we were exhausted, but relieved. At least the truck was packed. "All right, now let's unpack the truck!" WHAT? Every band had to unpack their trucks, being careful to keep the cases and large boxes we called coffins in order. Then, each band had stencils and white spray paint we used to number everything, so we would know what order and where to put each piece when we loaded up. As soon as we were done, we immediately re-loaded the truck—and now it was *really* late! However, our band's first gig was the next day—in Virginia. We had to pile in the van for a thirteen-hour drive, taking turns driving through the night, and we barely made our first show. "Welcome to Showcase!"

Wayne Hackett helps Pete Beal figure out where to begin loading the truck.

Each band assigned one person to be in charge of supervising unloading and loading the van. Working with the "roadie" students was also a key moment to connect and pour into impressionable young men, as some of our contributors experienced. Getting the job done with a fresh crew every stop required a lot of patience. Paul Turner and Dan Stankus both remember overzealous roadies disassembling their drum kits "nut by washer by bolt," doing their very best to help. With so many hands involved, it was easy to leave something behind, but sometimes costly to retrieve. If that happened, the person in charge of the "final check" had to call the principal and go back for it, which sometimes involved a very long drive. One of the "coffins" held the costumes for the Freedom Jam groups. Everyone had very colorful language to describe the stench permeating from that box. Hotel rooms and certainly the van all reeked with the sweat of guys that were leaving it all on the floor multiple times a day. Sunday was laundry day, the only day of relief from the odor. Being on the road was a life-changing experience, but not glamorous.

Day shows were more than just music performances. The goal was to engage and entertain, to connect with the audience, so each band performed carefully crafted moments that allowed them to bring students up on stage. Later we will elaborate on the "singing to the girl" moment, but several stories also talk about various comedy skits, which differed by band and year. During one or more of the comedy skits, band members would pull students, staff, and faculty up on stage, which sometimes led to some unexpected encounters.

» Connie Kolosey (1970-1980):

That year we stayed in Virginia with dips into West Virginia and Tennessee until Christmas time. At one point, we went to Harrisonburg High School. A couple of noteworthy things happened there. First, during the Star Wars skit, our front man Mike Loredo pulled a popular school athlete up on stage to play Darth Vader, along with a girl to play Princess Leah, a teacher as C3PO, and the class clown as R2D2 (note R2D2's costume consisted of a spaghetti strainer with a bike reflector light glued on). Mike chose a very, very tall kid named Ralph. Ralph was so tall his head grazed the curtain valance above the stage. Mike is about five foot seven. Mike asked, "What sport do you play?" as he held the mic up, his arm fully extended so that Ralph could speak into the mic. Ralph brought the house down and flustered the front man when, with a straight face, he said "football." As it turned out, Ralph Sampson grew to be seven foot four and eventually played for the NBA, winning numerous major honors. By 2012, he had been inducted into both the Naismith Memorial Basketball Hall of Fame and the National Collegiate Basketball Hall of Fame. Now Mr. Sampson is back in his hometown taking care of his community.

The other memorable event at Harrisonburg High School was that we met a high school senior named Lang Showalter (Bliss). Lang is a drummer and vocalist and was very interested in getting to know the band. He responded to the message about Jesus at the end of the show and began asking questions. The guys shared their faith with Lang. As the tour progressed, we kept in touch with Lang through letters (snail mail in those days) and he came out to see us in Charlotte, North Carolina, over spring break. On Easter Sunday, he made a commitment to Jesus. The next August, he joined Young American Showcase, and became an amazing performer and a dear friend to many Showcase members. We have remained friends all these years.

During that tour, we were in Washington, DC for Thanksgiving, where we played a couple of tough inner-city schools. Showcase always did better in rural areas and smaller towns where students had limited access to live rock and roll music. For Thanksgiving dinner we got dressed up and went to a fancy buffet at the Hilton. It was a real stretch to afford the $27 price tag on a $100 per week meal per diem. Mike Loredo recalls that he ate nine lobsters! "That was just the Mexican in me," he commented. "I can't let any buffet win!" After meals of fast food and late-night Denny's, the all-you-can-eat prime rib and lobster made us feel like we were on another planet. As we were laughing together and enjoying our road family, we looked over and saw a fellow rocker eating alone. The guys looked again and recognized David Gilmour from Pink Floyd. He looked lonely. The guys spoke to him and he was friendly and seemed glad for the company. We went home that night filled with food and gratitude for the blessing of each other.

Connie mentioned Lang Bliss and his amazing journey in her story. Next, in his own words, you can see the impact the groups had on the students, an effect that had little to do with their musical performance and everything to do with their character. Lang's story captures the magic formula that allowed this outrageous experiment, this crazy idea that was supposed to change students' lives, to work. Reading Lang's story, you can understand how important the formulas, the rules, the requirements, were, and how any deviation from those standards could cost the most valuable asset the groups and the company had—their reputation. Without that, principals would not allow the groups in, and the mission would be over as quickly as it began.

» Lang Bliss (1978-1984):

"Easter Song"

I was a senior at Harrisonburg High School in Virginia, when a band called Free Fare came to our school. I had just moved to that area the summer before, and remembered Free Fare playing at my previous high school. I thought that they were really cool, so when I found out that they were coming to this school, I asked to be the liaison for them. God was so in it. The band was the Kolosey Free Fare, who at the time consisted of John Phillips on guitar, Lee Murkey and Mike Loredo as front men, Dave Wagner on bass, Brooke Hopkins (keys), and Leo Watson (drums), managed by Gary and Connie Kolosey. The details of the time somewhat evade me, but there are things I do specifically remember. I remember thinking these were probably the nicest and coolest people I'd ever met. They seemed different, but I couldn't quite put my finger on what it was about them. I helped them to find the auditorium and all the other junk involved in a typical Free Fare setup, and I remember doing everything I could to hang out with them as long as I could. I think I managed to "liaise" with them almost the whole day.

I remember the bass player, Dave, taking an interest in me as I was messing around with playing bass as well as drums at the time, so we wrote back and forth after they left. He would send me bass exercises, so I practiced them. I can still remember them to this day. The night show came and they were doing some cool tunes. I remember them doing "September" by Earth, Wind & Fire, which was huge at the time. Also, "Hold the Line" by Toto had just come out and Brooke Hopkins took the time to teach me how to play it correctly (which I still remember to this day). They said that they were born-again Christians and I thought to myself, *That's it! That's what's so different about them!*

I thought about my church and the people I knew at church, but these "born-again Christians" were excited about life. They actually looked really cool and played great music; they had lives that displayed purpose, and, most important to this "unsaved" guy, they were kind and accepting of a dorky kid at a nowhere school in Nowhere, Virginia. I could not figure out why they would bother to give me the time of day, let alone make me feel like I fit right in with them. Connie and Gary were the coolest "older than me" people I had ever met and they seemed to really like me, which didn't really make sense, but I thought *I'll hang with 'em till they find out the truth of who I really am, and then they'll move on.* I thank God that they never did move on, even when they saw the real me! At one point, they said that maybe I could do this, too, when I graduated, and that was pretty much it for me. I was, from then on, in Showcase prep mode: "I will be in Free Fare...oh yes; I will be in Free Fare...."

Jumping ahead, Gary and Connie got permission to invite me to the band on the road over Easter week of my senior year. I took a Greyhound bus to Charlotte, North Carolina, and hung out with them for a week of shows, helping set up and attending the Bible studies every night before the show. Nobody, that I can remember, ever said to me, "Do you want to accept the Lord?" No one said anything of that nature, but I remember we ate at a Red Lobster, and the band had some wine for dinner. I wanted to keep the bottle as a keepsake. As I walked out of the restaurant, I began swaying and acting drunk, thinking they would all laugh. Gary quickly pulled me aside and said that it was not cool to do that, that they had a witness of being Christians and Christians did not act that way. I remember thinking that this was serious stuff; they really meant what they said and it made me respect them even more. Easter Sunday morning, I had to take the Greyhound back to Virginia and a life that I did not want nearly as much as what I had experienced with these people. I remember Easter morning so well; I was laying on the rollaway in the motel room, and it was pitch black (you know those hotel room-darkening curtains). The first thing I heard was some music on a boom box and the lyrics, "Hear the bells ringing, they're singing that you can be born again…" from "The Easter Song" by 2nd Chapter of Acts. The first thing I saw was the blinds opening and this beautiful sunshine pouring into the room. I truly felt then, and believe now, that God was pouring His love out on me, a seventeen-year-old, in an eternal moment intersecting with an earthly one.

Well, the band dropped me off at the bus station on their way to an Easter church service. I cried and didn't want to leave. It was so hard to go. I got on the bus and prepared for the ride back to Harrisonburg. I prayed to accept Jesus into my heart, by myself, on the bus. I couldn't contain the sense of huge weights falling off me, and an insuppressible joy! For the next nine hours, at every bus stop in every little town between Charlotte and Harrisonburg, I grabbed Christian tracts and pamphlets out of the little metal racks on the walls of those bus stations and read everything I could about Jesus and my new faith. Finally, because I felt like I was going to burst if I didn't tell somebody, I tapped a woman on the shoulder in front of me who looked like she wouldn't slug me if I told her something weird, and said to her, "I just became a born-again Christian!" She didn't slug me and she said, "So am I. I'm a Mennonite." To Gary and Connie, Dave, Lowell and Barb Lytle, and everyone else involved in Showcase at the time, thank you! It was your commitment to Jesus that so attracted me, that so fascinated me, and that you included me when I wasn't "one of you," that gave me no other choice but to also fall in love with the Savior you so excellently represented. I love you all. He has risen!

Lang Bliss selling posters after a night show at Licking Valley High School, Newark, Ohio

Lang's story also illustrates that introducing someone to a new life in Christ often requires more than a few minutes at the end of a show; often we have to hear the same message repeatedly—see it lived out in others as evidence of its truth—before we finally pay attention and make a change. We are watching. "Is this for real?" we ask. We will notice if your actions do not line up with your words. We will see immediately if your faith is not genuine, if it is just a well-practiced sales pitch. While the Holy Spirit is working in us, Satan is casting doubt. Our family and friends, our history, may all be working against us; we are so vulnerable. This is why the Showcase organization did the best it could to test the spiritual foundation of each band and staff member before allowing them in. This is why "the rules" were put into place. It was too important; too much was at stake. This was just as true for staff members as it was for musicians.

Rule #4: No one on staff who does not have a personal relationship with Jesus. *The reason for this rule was clear: to be part of the leadership team you had to share the same passion for the mission of the company, and you could not do that without the same spiritual foundation. Even though Lowell had a strict policy of only hiring those who already had a relationship with Jesus Christ, on occasion, candidates would be less than honest about their faith. Sometimes, Lowell would make the decision to bring someone in on a temporary basis only. Almost always, that person would find their way to God, as the following stories illuminate:*

» Gary Kopco (1972–1978):

From Soldier to Saved

> *"For God hath not appointed us to wrath,*
> *but to obtain salvation by our Lord Jesus Christ."*

In 1971, I returned home from Vietnam as a war-hardened twenty-one-year-old army officer. During the previous year, as a very young infantry platoon leader and company commander, I led up to 125 men at a time into life and death situations, with results that would impact me for the rest of my life. How often would I remember the aftermath of an event where lives were lost and men were wounded or disfigured for life, and ask myself, "For what?"

In my earlier years, as a practicing Catholic youth, I had no reason to doubt my faith nor delve into spiritual matters such as who God really was and what He truly intended for me. Now I had questions, but no answers, about a God that would allow a twenty-one-year-old young man to be a leader of men in wartime and to experience horrors counterintuitive to Christian thinking.

Upon my release from the military in late 1971, I enjoyed my new life back in the "real world" and decided to take a Christmas holiday rest before looking for a job. In early 1972, a musician friend from my youth contacted me and told me to expect a call from a man he was currently working for in the musical/entertainment field. He was looking for a drummer to replace an injured player in one of several bands that he had formed to travel the country playing top 40 music, interspersed with comedy routines for high school assembly programs. A few days later, my phone rang, and a man with a deep voice introduced himself as Lowell Lytle with Young American Showcase in Pinellas Park, Florida. He asked if I would meet with him to explore the possibility of a short-term stint as the drummer for his group currently touring New England. While we did not discuss specifics, I was intrigued, and we met two days later at his home.

At our meeting, this very friendly man explained their performance methods and schedule, then told me the reason that he founded his company of five touring bands. "Here's the twist," he explained. "During the evening program, we deliver a Christian message of salvation, of receiving eternal life through acceptance of Jesus Christ as Lord and Savior." Noting the confused look on my face, he quickly continued. "Listen; while I sense that you have not taken this step of faith in your life, I have an immediate need for a drummer for just two months, and I'm willing to consider this a business arrangement."

Consider the people God brings to you with the same grace God had when He was considering you. Listen to God, and be open.

Figuring that I did not have much to lose and it would be nice seeing New England in the spring, I said, "Sure, let's do it." Two days later, I was shaking hands with my new band-mates in a motel room outside of Boston. That night we were rehearsing the program and I was scrambling to learn the show that we would be performing the very next morning. As the days went by, I learned more about the entertainment program, the musical skill level of the band, and the spiritual walk of band members. On all three counts, I was impressed with what this band was accomplishing. However, there was one band member in particular whose spiritual walk got my attention. Every morning he would get up a bit earlier than the others, pull out his Bible, and read his passages for the day. While I would have said that he was the least talented of the group and more laid back than dynamic, I was drawn to his quiet spirit and walk. I asked questions about his Christian faith; he would share biblical principles with me, with no pressure to pray for salvation. Over the next two months, I listened to the daily delivery of God's message of salvation in our concerts, and the influence of these talented musicians put me under conviction.

When the tour ended, so did my short stint with Young American Showcase. I returned home to Sarasota, Florida, and while I was beginning to move on with my life, I could not avoid the "still small voice" of God telling me the time was right for me to join the family of God. In June of 2002, late one night, I couldn't sleep. Physically, as well as mentally, I felt the pressure to make a decision. It was that night I prayed the Sinner's Prayer and accepted Jesus Christ as my personal Lord and Savior.

The editors know that, by now, you have heard this transformational story from different people, in different circumstances, from different sides of the conversation, but with something in common. A person sees something different in another, something they are drawn to. They learn that difference has something to do with faith in Jesus. They are not preached at, proselytized, or made to feel anything but loved and accepted where they are, and for who they are. This is another part of "earning the right to be heard"—one you cannot skip over. There are no shortcuts. Once you have someone's attention, once they know that "thing" they are attracted to is Jesus, that's where the fun part begins. In these cases, Lang, Gary, and others experienced something internally. We call this the work of the Holy Spirit. God does His thing, and before you know it, they are asking Jesus to be their Lord and Savior. We will talk more about this later. For now, we know that some of you reading have no idea what we are talking about. Please, just keep reading.

After Gary became a believer and began to grow spiritually, he rejoined Young American Showcase, and over five years worked both on the road and eventually as national booking director. We are going to pivot now and introduce you to another key leader in the organization, Lance Abair. Many of the stories in this book refer to Lance, who was "love and energy" personified, and the person in charge of teaching rookies during rehearsal camp how to earn the right to be heard through their performance. Lowell first met this one-of-a-kind individual while Lance was with The Entertainers, a spirited and highly successful group that had performed with all of the big name entertainers in Tahoe. While Lowell was working to get four bands on the road, God was busy maneuvering Lance's circumstances to prepare him to play an incredibly important role in the company. We point this out to you because, as you are inspired to begin your own radical experiment in evangelism, or in serving God's purposes in any number of other capacities, we want to remind you that your plans are no secret to God. If He is in it, you can guarantee He is at work, and has been, getting things, and people, in place. Your job is the same as we find in Joshua 1:9 when God sent Joshua into the harshest, most frightening of situations:

"Have I not commanded you? Be strong and courageous. Do not be afraid, do not be discouraged, for the Lord your God will be with you wherever you go." (NIV)

When Lance first came to YAS, he worked on a temporary basis just like Gary, simply because he did not have that all-important relationship with Jesus. From Lowell, we see how he and Lance first met. First, Lowell describes one of the difficulties they had in the early rehearsal camps:

"We could teach routines and music, and we could set ground rules, but in just a couple of weeks, it was much harder to teach a group of guys who had never met before how to entertain, capture the audience, work as a unit, and win the right to deliver the gospel."

[Through a circumstance one could only categorize as God-ordained, Lowell saw Lance perform in a group called "The Fabulous Entertainers." Lowell describes the scene:]

"When we walked into the place, I couldn't believe it. The band was playing the song 'I Wanna Take You Higher,' and there was so much energy on that stage that the audience could not sit still. People in their fifties and sixties were standing on chairs and tables. It was amazing!" [Lowell convinced Lance, the leader of the band, to come down to rehearsal camp for three days to teach his bands how to perform. A few months after those fateful three days, The Fabulous Entertainers broke up and Lance found himself suddenly out of the industry he loved. God was setting the stage. In his own words, Lance talks about that transformation as only Lance can.]

» Lance Abair (1972-1983):

The Holy Spirit did a tap dance on my head

The Entertainers had broken up and I was selling motor homes in the hot sun of St. Petersburg, Florida. I lasted for about five weeks of that and had to quit. I don't believe in lying. After paying long dues, the fact that it could all just go poof hit me hard. It didn't seem fair.

I remembered spending a couple of days with some young musicians the summer before to show them some entertainment ropes. It was fun. Finding myself out of work with a wife and young daughter, I called Lowell to see if he needed some help with the bands on a more permanent basis. He told me that he couldn't bring me into the company because "I wasn't a member of the family." I knew they were Christians but I didn't hold that against them. So, Lowell ended up hiring me just for the summer camp.

When I got down to rehearsal camp, they were handing out "Reach Out" books (the New Testament from the Living Bible). I asked if I could have one and they said yes. I was surprised to find a Bible that you could actually read and understand. The words came in. During those weeks, there were Bible studies I also attended. I had questions, and they had answers. I'm a curious person. About three weeks into camp, I was walking down to one of the practice rooms in the evening and all of a sudden, it hit me that this was all for real, not a fairy tale. I knew I had to buy into this, but had no idea how to go about it. I stopped in my tracks, asked where Lowell was, and mentioned that I needed to take care of business "now!" Wayne Hackett, Lowell, and I'm not sure who else ended up meeting me at a bench outside on the campus that night, and I asked what I needed to do. They explained stuff to me and asked if I wanted to pray for salvation. I said "yes"—and I did! When it was finished, I felt good about it and went on with camp. That weekend I went home to St. Pete to see my family, and told my wife, Linda, about what I had learned and what had taken place. She told me that the same thing happened to her! We were *both* saved. Essentially, the Holy Spirit had done a tap dance on both our foreheads. At last, I knew why I was put on earth, and it made sense.

Lance approached his newfound faith like everything else—he poured himself into learning as much as he could, as quickly as he could. As he grew spiritually, he was brought on board with YAS, shaping green musicians into powerhouses that could "earn the right to be heard," making sure they had the best equipment to work with by securing sponsorships, recruiting new band members, and, among other duties, going out on the road to critique bands and help them improve. His uncompromising enthusiasm and boldness were essential to a young woman he met on the road who, like his wife, was also named "Linda."

» Linda Miller (1976-1978):

Groupie meets the Gospel
God used YAS to help this nice Jewish girl come to know Jesus, by having Free Fare groups come to my hometown three years in a row. It was unheard of to have different groups play an area three consecutive years, since standard practice was never to book a group back into an area without a couple-year break.

I was a senior at Grant High in Portland, Oregon when the Hornyak Free Fare ('72 -'73) came to town and did a show at my school. My three girlfriends and I became "friends" of the band (yes, I will admit, we were groupies) and went to all of their shows throughout the city. As we spent time with the group, there were conversations about God and being a Christian, but when the band left, so did my thoughts about Jesus. I mean, I was Jewish, for goodness sake! However, God wasn't done with me yet.

The very next year, King Free Fare ('73–'74) showed up in Portland. By this time, I was a college freshman. Bobby King, the manager, had been the bass player with the Hornyak Free Fare the year before, so my friends and I already knew him and went to see a couple of shows and go to dinner. We had several conversations about God and I got that knot in my stomach again, but when the group left the area, so did my Jesus search. *[The editors have to smile at the consistency of these young men, year after year, show after show. A group of beautiful young college women meet them for dinner after what we already know was an exhausting day. Instead of simply relaxing and enjoying "a night off," the gospel conversations continued—gentle, accepting, patient, but consistent. This is why the bands were there.]*

The third year (my second in college) the Hardley Free Fare ('74–'75) arrived and played the Portland and Seattle areas for a couple months. Somehow, my girlfriends found out about their shows in the area, so I came home for the weekend to go. Lance Abair was out visiting the group, so I got the chance to meet him. I will never forget sitting in an auditorium after one of the shows and having Lance (who was so intimidating) ask me why it was taking me so long to make a decision about Jesus—he knew this was the third group I had hung out with. He told me straight out that he was sure that "God is going to do a tap dance on your forehead" so I might as well quit fighting it. I was offended and angry that he would talk to me that way and did everything I could to avoid him the rest of the evening.

The next day the group was going to spend the day at the Oregon Coast and invited us girls to go with them. By now, I was totally smitten with Steve Thomas, so there was no way I was going to miss it. We were all going to make the ninety-minute drive together in the YAS truck and the Hardleys' car. I maneuvered things to make sure I would not have to ride in the same vehicle as Lance, but after Steve, Pete, my friend, and I climbed into the truck, in came Lance. I was on edge the entire day waiting for Lance to start lecturing me again, but Lance, in his wisdom, never said a word. By the end of the day I was such a wreck from waiting to see what Lance was going to do, that I brought up the subject of God myself. I sat in tears telling Lance that I felt God pulling me but I was afraid and confused. What would my family say? How could I be a traitor to Judaism and accept that Jesus was the Messiah? Accepting Jesus went against everything I had believed. Lance was gentle and said that I needed to find out for myself. He told me to get a Living Bible and start reading it, and pray that God Himself would show me whether it was true or not.

So, that's what I did. I went back to college, got the biggest hard cover Living Bible you have ever seen, and started reading it, praying and asking God to tell me if it was true. Several passages ended up hitting me in the face and I realized it was true: Jesus was God's Son and I wanted Him in my life. I went to Portland for the weekend with my cousin (who was one of the girls in our little groupie group) and, together, we prayed and accepted the Lord. After that, I went home to Portland whenever I could to join the other girls and hang out with the band.

I planned to keep my conversion from my family for at least six months; as you can imagine, I was apprehensive about how that conversation would go over. But God had other plans, and through a series of events my parents soon found out that I'd become a Christian. They were upset to say the least, and immediately pulled me out of college. They brought me back to Portland, where they felt they would have a chance to change my mind, to have me talk to a rabbi who could show me what nonsense Jesus was.

Linda certainly had a rough beginning in her faith, immediately tested and isolated from those who could help her grow in her newfound faith. We will see later that this situation, also, was all part of God's larger design, but in the meantime, it points out a larger problem. Students were responding to the gospel every night, with every band, across the country, every year. Linda mentioned bands were usually not booked in the same school or city two years in a row. Students would more typically experience one amazing show in their teens, perhaps two, and hear an unexpected and powerful testimony. They were given an opportunity to respond by writing on their tickets and turning them in. The tickets of those who indicated an interest in Christianity, or who actually asked Jesus into their hearts that night, were forwarded to the Billy Graham organization for follow-up—by the thousands. Across the years, millions of students had this shared experience, and tens of thousands per year responded, across twenty-two years. This radical experiment was working, better than anyone could have imagined. So, naturally, wherever you see God working, you also see Satan doing everything in his power to interrupt the work.

POSTER GALLERY

Each band had face posters they sold at concerts. Following are many of those posters, promo shots, and band posters, with as many names (and additional photos) as we could add.

Terry Casburn, Lowell Lytle, Joe Brown,
First Free Fare
Gary Horton, Wayne Hackett & Henry

SHALOM
Bobby King
Tom Green
Wayne Hackett

FREE FARE

From Top, Left to Right: Dave Ayers, Sim Kilpatrick, Hiroshi Upshur, Robert McDevitt, Justin Smith, Randy Copeland, Keith Conley, Nathan Steele

FREE FARE
Hiroshi Upshur
Steve Thomas Ritchie Ray
Pete Beal

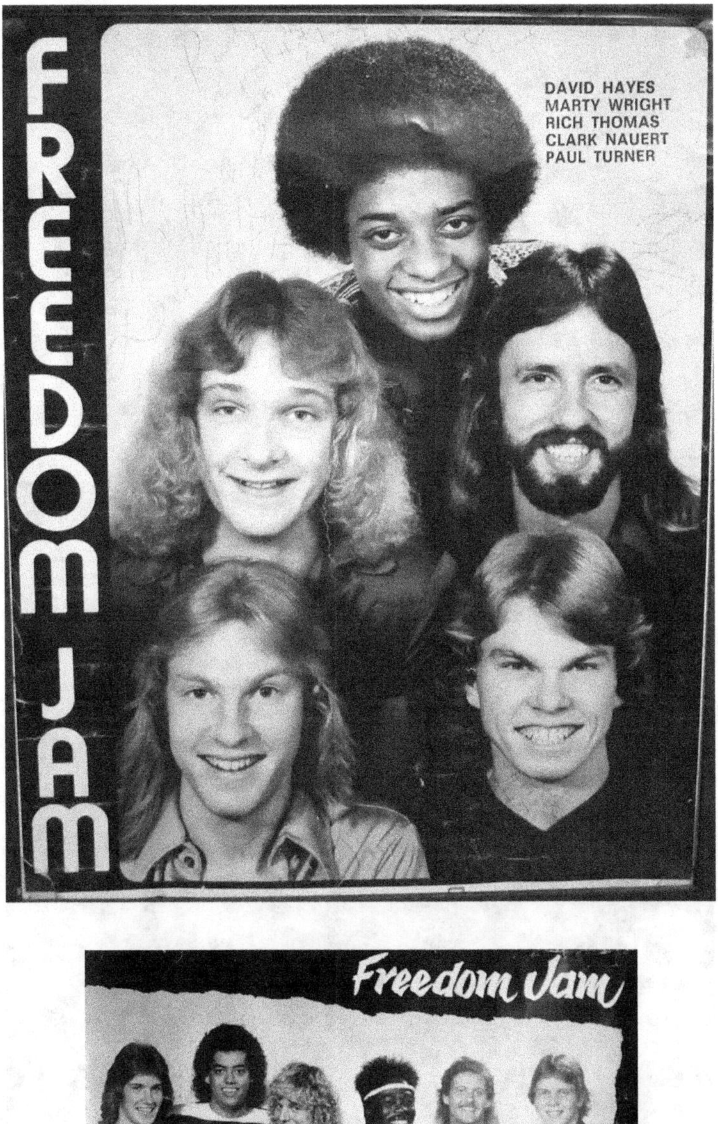
FREEDOM JAM
DAVID HAYES
MARTY WRIGHT
RICH THOMAS
CLARK NAUERT
PAUL TURNER

Freedom Jam
TONY LECLERC
LENNY BROOKS
TRACY DUARTE
ISAK DILLARD
MARK WARFEL
BILL VINCENT

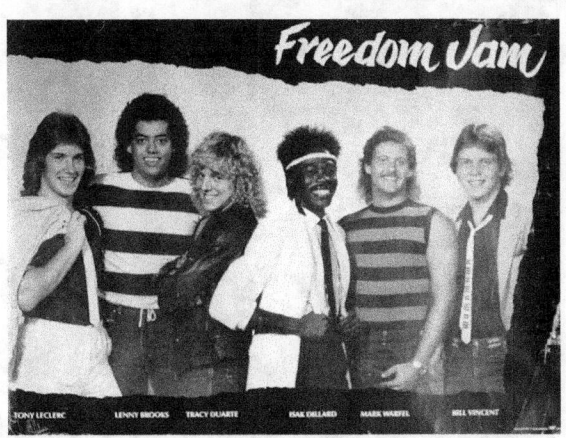

Brad McCarter   Chad Miller   Troy Stone   Doug Webber   Mike Bingol   Dave Frischkorn

IAN MICHAELS   RODD WILSON   SCOTT GILBERTSON   IKE DILLARD   RICK JANTS   MIKE SMITH

Joel Weaver   Joel Panganiban   Justin Fox   Corey Stark   Chris Clark

?   ?   Dave Fiorazo   Steve Tanner   Steve Laurence

John Gunsett   Ed Shephard   Jimmy Arceneaux   Brian Zwahlen

Tony LeClerc Brian Zwahlen Joel Johnson Don Sanders ?

Tony LeClerc Lenny Brooks Tracy Duarte Isaac Dillard Mark Warfel ?

Bret Pemelton J R Montgomery Danny Moore Steve Tanner ?

Ricky Rhinehart   Roger Nichols   Glenn Quiggins   Greg Motyka   Tom Caffey

Terry Rieff   Chris Lundquist   Dave Walker   Tyrone Banks   Sam Salvo   Chad Matson

Chuck Sarchione   ?   Mark Smith   Tyrone Banks   ?

PART FOUR

RISK AND REWARD

Lowell: *It's always darkest right before it goes completely black.*

When you are in the midst of a radical experiment, risk comes with the territory. You cannot eliminate it. You can mitigate it, but risk will always be there. Trust that God will always be there, also, and do not let the risk deter you from the mission. Did God keep a graceful hand of protection over these road warriors? Read along and tell us what you think.

Over and over again, bands saw that each school was a divine appointment, and sometimes God would go to extraordinary lengths to get them there. In fact, sometimes it was a miracle they arrived at all, as Joe Brown and Bobby Flake's stories illustrated for us earlier. There were many road incidents and war stories from all of the driving each band did. With such a tight schedule, getting lost was easy—and potentially disastrous. Being pulled over was always a challenge, as highway patrol officers and local police were usually very suspicious of a van packed with mysterious boxes and four to five longhaired young men. The occasional accident or lapse of judgement was inevitable, but miraculously, no one, across more than two decades, encompassing about 150 separate tours and well over three million miles, was ever seriously injured.

Radical experiments will always include risk.
Be smart, but don't be deterred.

» Monty Godfrey (1985-1988):

Number One Rule

One of the rules of the road was that two people must be awake while driving the company vehicle. Let me be more specific—it was the NUMBER ONE RULE! As people that toured with me may remember, I preferred driving to being a passenger. I usually did not have to lobby to drive since the highway was an excellent place to get a nap, as we were, if nothing else, sleep-deprived in those days.

This particular night, we were leaving a show in Orlando and had to be in North Carolina for a few shows en route to New York. It was very late and I did not have driving duties for some reason. So, I took on the ever-important role of the navigator, whose sole existence was to make sure we were on course, and see that the driver stayed awake and alert. To set the stage, four guys are asleep in the back of the truck while the driver and I are in front. The sleeping guys trust that the two in the front are following Rule NUMBER ONE!

If one of the guys up front starts to nod off, you really want it to be the driver. The ever-alert navigator (me in this case), would be there to save the day. This is the part of the story where I fall on the proverbial sword...

As we were driving north on I-95 near St. Augustine around 1 a.m., I was jarred awake as the truck was tipping over on its side. My arm was going through the glass of the passenger door as it hit the pavement doing at least fifty miles per hour. We slid on the pavement for about twenty to thirty feet. I am lucky my arm was not crushed in the process. The driver had (allegedly) nodded off and over-corrected the steering wheel as he was veering off the side of the highway. The result was our thirty-foot truck, on its side, occupying BOTH lanes of the interstate, with the underside of the truck facing oncoming traffic. Of course, the underside of the truck is basically black, and there were no lights or reflective glass that would give approaching vehicles much warning in the dead of night. I remember hearing tires screeching and seeing cars, which had narrowly avoided collision, off to the side of the road. Amazingly, no one hit us. No one hit any other vehicles. There were no other accidents, no one else was hurt, and those of us in the truck were able to get out safely and suffered only minor injuries. The truck was totaled, although most of the gear was not harmed. I will never forget that event.

» Glenn Quiggins (1982-1983):

Lowell, the Vikings, and our Guardian Angel

I remember Lowell came up to see us and took the band to the Hubert Humphrey Metrodome to see Tampa Bay play the Vikings. It was September 12, 1982, 58,000-plus fans, and snowing so much it started to cave in the dome a bit. This was my first NFL game and it was a great time, except the Bucs lost 17-10. Another night we were on our way to a show, where Lowell was waiting for us. We were leaving this little town and getting ready to hit the interstate, when both of the wheels on the left rear side broke off and passed us going down the road! We skidded to a stop as we watched our wheels roll into the back yard of someone's cookout. Our guardian angel was watching over us, as we had not made it to the interstate yet, and nobody was hurt. The neighbors helped us find a mechanic and we were on the road again in no time! The show must go on!

» Jeff Siebert (1989-1991):

Diesel Dive

You just never know how dangerous driving the Showcase trucks can be. I was driving down the Pennsylvania Turnpike. There were banks of snow on both sides of us when the guy next to me said, "You know these things are diesel engines, they run off the compression. In fact, you don't even need a key once they're started."

"Really?" I responded. He assured me it was true, so I turned the key and pulled it out of the ignition. Everything seemed fine. "Yeah, you're right!" All of a sudden, I heard a *click*, and the wheel locked up!

Just a few of the wreck shots. These photos and the stories ahead help illustrate how miraculous it was that no one across twenty-two years was ever killed, or even seriously injured or hospitalized from these road incidents. Next, read the story of this burned-out hulk, from Matthew Phillips.

We are on the interstate going sixty miles per hour. My hand is shaking. I am so nervous I can't get the key back into the slot. Now we are headed right for the snowbank, and we hit it full force. FLUFF! At least it stopped us.

» Matthew Phillips (1984-1985):

Reverse at 60 mph

This was the Freedom Jam 1985 Alaska Tour. We were two weeks out of rehearsal camp and crossing Colorado. I was sitting in the front suicide seat when it happened.

The driver was our bass player, out of the flatlands of Texas. He was so excited to see the first mountain range on our journey off in the distance. He raised his arm and pointed, saying, "LOOK AT ALL the mountains!" His forearm caught the column shifter, moving it from "Drive" to "Reverse"—at sixty miles per hour. No sound. No nothing. But, we knew that it was bad.

Tracy shifted back into "D," gave it some gas—no engine response, so we coasted over to the side of the highway and jumped out. Roger looked underneath the engine and noticed a few little drops of fire, minutes later, dripping from the engine to the road.

We yanked everything out of the front of the truck, then the fire began raging! We opened the back and threw out all of our gear. People were pulling over to help us move everything off to the side of the road as the whole thing went up.

The volunteer fire department eventually showed up from the next town and helped to stop traffic and hose it down. All our gear and equipment was saved, thanks to Roger. We rented a U-Haul truck and I don't think we missed a single show. The next Showcase truck we got had a cracked engine block. THAT was the REAL nightmare!

» Stan Arthur (1977-1990):

Steep Downgrade Ahead

It was only a four-piece band, led by manager Dave Mikulsky, with Donny Bogtong on guitar, David Payton (who we called Doc) on bass, Skeeter Barkley on keyboards, and me as the drummer/front man. Our tour took us to the Maritime provinces of Canada, starting with a month in Nova Scotia followed by a couple of weeks in Newfoundland (pronounced NEW-fin-land). We traveled by ferryboat from Sydney, Nova Scotia, to Port aux Basques and began our journey across a province that was about 90 percent frozen wasteland in the month of February 1980. From the map above, you can see a bright green line that is something like nine hundred kilometers from Port aux Basques to St. John's. It's a nine-hour drive. We worked our way to St. John's, having three shows in that area, before our last few days in Newfoundland working our way back to Port aux Basques and the ferry ride back to Nova Scotia. Our last show ended at 9 p.m. on a Thursday.

During the concert, a wet, clumpy snow had begun to fall. We had another show scheduled for Friday morning, retracing our journey back up Route 1 about three hundred kilometers. I began to fear that it was going to be a treacherous journey on an empty road with no sleep at the other end. The driving conditions would require that we maintain a speed of no more than thirty-five miles per hour, making for a six-to-seven hour trip. During the pack-up, I had seen Manager Dave with a road map in his hands, chatting with two of the stage crew guys. Once we were all packed up and ready to depart, I got behind the wheel. Dave hopped aboard the large GMC step van and announced that we now had a shortcut from the school back to Route 1 that would shave a full hour off our trip. Hurray for that! However, things did not go as planned. As we hit the road, it became apparent soon enough that we were in trouble due to the wet snow, what with tires spinning on the pavement and our rear end fishtailing a bit here and there. Many of the road signs were already covered in snow and unreadable. Somehow, we managed to find the little two-lane road the stage crew had told us about, so with a fair amount of trepidation, I made the turn and began that leg of the journey.

Before long, I realized that we were headed up a twisty-turny mountain range with a wall of rock on one side, a sheer drop on the other, and nothing but a flimsy guardrail keeping us from plunging to our deaths. For at least thirty minutes, we continued to climb up and up and up, still fishtailing from tires that really were not gripping the road at all. To say I was frightened would be understating my state of mind significantly. I tried using the high beams to see farther ahead what sort of twisty turn the road would take next but they only reflected off the heavy snow that was coming down, making it impossible to see the road. After a long, white-knuckled stretch of highway, things were about to get worse. I remember the road straightening and flattening out a bit and then seeing a large yellow road sign almost completely obscured by snow, making it impossible to read. Almost immediately, it became apparent what the sign surely must have warned: STEEP DOWNGRADE AHEAD.

This was going to be bad and I knew it. The fishtailing and tire spinning got worse as the twists and turns in the road became more intense. Now I was gently pumping the brake pedal to keep from accelerating completely out of control and plummeting to our doom. I was terrified. My bandmates were well aware of the danger judging by the sounds that were coming from behind me. I'm not sure but I think our manager, Dave, might have actually been asleep up in the bunk. This went on and on for what seemed like an hour but was surely only ten minutes before, thankfully, I could see the road flattening and straightening in front of us under the light of a full moon. I'm sure I said something like, "We're going to be fine now," as I focused on just slowing the truck down before anything else happened.

I observed that the shoulders on both sides of the road were piled high, perhaps five feet more, with snow and ice banks from the snowplows that had cleared this road during the winter. I knew that we would be reaching Route 1 at any moment, making everything all right. Just then, I could make out dimly just ahead the Route 1 junction. Then all hope of this episode ending well drained from me as I realized there was a sharp thirty-degree right turn just before the intersection. I hit the brakes hard, locking the wheels, and turned the steering wheel all the way but it was no use. I shouted, "We're not going to make it!" as the truck swung sideways on the road. The truck slammed into the roadside snow bank flatly on its left side, becoming airborne for just a moment before hitting the rocky field on the other side. At the moment of impact, the windshields and the side door windows exploded in a shower of tiny glass cubes. The four-foot- long Naugahyde-covered piece of plywood we called the suicide seat hit me hard on my right shoulder as my head slammed into the left wall. The truck came to rest on its left side with the headlights still brilliantly illuminating the Route 1 junction that lay no more than fifty yards in front of us.

We had come so close after such a terrifying trip. The first thing I remember was having the wind knocked out of me and trying to breathe. I could hear the moans and groans coming from the guys behind me. After a few seconds, I managed to ask, "Is everyone alright?" The next thing I heard was Dave's muffled cry coming from the bunk that had folded in on him, trapping him. "Get me out of here!" He had landed on his head during the impact. Donny was emphatically asking over and over if everyone was okay. Not only had everyone survived, but we were relatively unscathed. There were no broken bones or bloody wounds needing medical attention, which was miraculous, considering the force of the impact.

We needed emergency help but in 1980, there were no mobile phones, and we were deep into the wilderness of Newfoundland now. Dave and I decided to walk the short distance up to Route 1 and have a look around. The others bundled up and made themselves as comfortable as possible. When we got to the highway, we looked left and right trying to determine which way to go. If we started walking south, it would be back toward St John's, but that was very far away. We looked north and could barely make out a dim glow on the horizon, suggesting that civilization would be more likely in that direction—so we began walking. We walked a distance of what we later were told was more than four miles when we came upon a phosphate processing plant that was the size of a small city, brightly lit with powerful halogen lamps by the hundreds indicating this was a twenty-four-hour operation.

We walked up to the security shack and told the guard what had happened. He snapped into action, picking up the phone. Within minutes, others arrived and took us immediately to a large cafeteria, providing blankets and hot coffee. It turned out that we were not far from a small community where these workers all lived. Without our knowledge, someone made some calls and more people got involved in helping us. A big white Dodge van showed up to take us back to the crash site and collect our bandmates. An on-site mechanic with a huge diesel wrecker followed behind us. The others referred to this man as "crazy," meaning that he wasn't afraid of anything. Judging by the deep scars on his face, I assumed that was no exaggeration. Somehow, he was able to wrap the tow truck cable around our vehicle and pull it upright back onto its wheels! From there, he pulled the step van up onto Route 1 and towed it back to the plant. We were taken to a motel that had a very large room upstairs, with four beds and a cot that had somehow already been prepared for us. It turned out that the men who appeared on the scene to help were all members of the local Jehovah's Witness church, and were deeply compelled to do this good work when the opportunity presented itself.

My memories of the morning after are pretty fuzzy. I was hurting badly by that time, with a bump on my head and a badly bruised shoulder and arm where the suicide seat struck me. I do know that Dave went to see the step van in daylight to survey the damage. The truck body was slightly askew from its short flight to the rocks, but amazingly enough, it was still drivable. The left side was badly scarred from sliding a few feet on the rocks after landing. Dave paid Mr. Crazy Tow Truck Man to drive it all the way back to St. John's where there was an auto glass shop ready and waiting to cut custom glass to fit the now imperfectly shaped windows. As impossible as it sounds, we were able to get back on the road in our newly scarred-up step van by 7 p.m. that day. We missed only one show that could not be made up due to our ferryboat reservation that was only a few days later. That same step van lasted us two more months back in the US before the rear end went completely out. I believe Tom Miller drove a new step van from Florida to replace it. I remember the relief of not having to drive that battle-scarred road warrior vehicle into school parking lots anymore. As we have discussed, first impressions are lasting. In the end, we were all struck by how well we survived that night. God had shielded us from serious harm and death with just enough protection to see us through and allow us to continue the mission. We continued to give Him thanks in our prayers. I know that only His grace and mercy could have spared us from far worse that surely would have happened had He not covered us with His love.

Bands and home office staff had no shortage of stories to tell about teens whose lives were dramatically changed by the work of Young American Showcase.

Students could easily see these guys were genuine, and were working their hearts out for them. The bands earned the right to be heard, and the students listened and responded to their gospel message. The response was worth the risk. Still, a tremendous amount of work had to happen before a band ever rolled up to a gymnasium. Well ahead of each band's tour schedule, a booker had been there before them, lining up the gigs, the motels, mapping routes, planning every detail. Bookers often went out alone or with their spouses. The next two stories illustrate their work. First, Valorie McNabb Pope, the first female booker to hit the road for YAS. Valorie traveled alone—sort of. In 1985, as she worked her way across Newfoundland, Canada, booking and setting up a tour schedule, Valorie also had trouble on the road, along with a good dose of almighty protection.

» Valorie McNabb Pope (1982-1988):

Newfoundland Angel

I was booking in Newfoundland, part of which is a mountainous island off the east coast of Canada, accessible only by a ten- to twelve-hour ferry ride from Nova Scotia, which lies just off the eastern tip of Maine. I had been able to visit with one of the bands somewhere in the hinterlands of Newfoundland and was trying to get back to Newark, New Jersey, to pick up Lowell's daughter, Debbie. We were going to meet up with two Showcase bands in NYC for the Macy's Thanksgiving Day Parade and a meal. Because the Nova Scotia ferry departed only at 12:00 noon and 12:00 midnight, I learned to be not just "on time" but early, both to ensure space for my vehicle on the ferry and to avoid a twelve-hour wait.

Several weeks earlier, I had crossed Cabot Strait on the ferry to take care of business appointments from the west coast of Newfoundland to St. John's, the capital, located on the province's east coast. I was traveling with my trusty companion, a mixed-breed terrier rescue pup named LG (short for "Life Guard"). She was a champion!

Having finished my business in St. John's, I began the ten-hour drive back to the west coast of the island, and the ferry that would take me back to Sydney, Nova Scotia. From there I planned to drive along the New England coast to get to Newark. Excited to get on with my journey, I made one last stop to gas up before beginning a section of the highway where there would be no opportunities for food, drink, or fuel.

Pay Attention to Warnings

The attendant in the fuel station warned me about incoming weather and cautioned me to be on the lookout for the occasional moose or two. Fueled with gasoline, coffee, and a candy bar, I set out to reach the ferry landing in time for the midnight ferry. I was determined! If I didn't make that ferry, I would have to wait in my car for the next available ferry at noon the following day. Not fun.

About thirty minutes later, it began to snow. Further down the road, I did indeed have an encounter with a moose who did not want to move off the highway—but I won that battle! However, the snow began falling much heavier and the wind began to gust harder and harder. Eventually, I knew I was going to have to pull off the road because of near-zero visibility, and winds so great they were pushing my car around on the road, making it unsafe to drive. As a solo female driver, I had serious doubts about pulling off the highway in the middle of nowhere. Concerns about being hit and having truckers approach me to "help" just did not seem prudent. So, I cautiously continued.

That was when it happened.

A powerful burst of wind hit my car, pushing it sideways towards the shoulder, and at that point, I realized I would not be able to stop. I turned the wheel, positioning the nose of the car to face the edge of the road, and began sliding as the wind forced the car down the side of the cliff toward a rocky ravine. After what seemed like an eternity, I came to a stop—about thirty feet below the road. I rolled down the window and looked out, back up toward the highway. I couldn't see anything because of the whiteout conditions.

Day 2—Hopeless

While my situation did seem hopeless, I knew I would be fine if I just stayed right where I was. I had access to my coat, and the rest of my clothes, which I could layer around me. I knew I wouldn't freeze. Plus, I had my dog and a candy bar! I decided to leave my headlights on and the hazard lights flashing, and began to play my favorite music. I thought I might as well make it a party, right? I was determined to make the best of it and have a positive attitude.

I turned sideways on the front seat, propped up my feet, and unpacked my clothes layering them over LG and myself. We settled in for what we thought would be an overnight stay as we waited for dawn and a chance to climb up the rocks to get help.

[While faith and a positive spirit can certainly get you a long way, Valorie was in more danger than she realized. Weather reports for that day showed accumulating snow, a steady twenty mile-per-hour wind with gusts exceeding fifty miles per hour, and the temperature that night would drop to below 26 degrees, not accounting for wind chill. Hypothermia, even protected by a car, layers of clothes, and a little dog, could easily begin to set in within thirty minutes, and could be deadly. As if her current situation wasn't bad enough, the storm was about to get significantly worse. Valorie did not realize how much help she really needed, and how quickly she would need it. Of course, God knew.]

About fifteen minutes after I burrowed down for the night ahead, I was completely shocked when, from out of nowhere, someone knocked on the side window right where I had propped my head. Needless to say, I was startled. I jumped, and LG began barking furiously.

I rolled down the window just a little, and a small-statured, older man motioned that he would like me to get out of the car. He pointed up the ravine and indicated he would help me. I decided this might be one time when I really would like to accept a ride from a stranger. I shut off the car's lights, grabbed my purse and my dog, and up the rocks we went. Now, understand, the wind gusts and snow still made this climb practically impossible, but somehow we managed.

How did this guy find me?

When we were in the man's vehicle—an old army jeep—I asked him how in the world he even knew to look for me. He explained that he had been at the fuel stop, had noticed I was from Florida, and had seen my headlights behind him until the wind started gusting. At that point, he pulled over to make sure I was still coming down the highway.

When he never saw my vehicle again, he knew something had probably happened, and came back to look. He had a spotlight attached to his vehicle, but couldn't see anything, but then there was a quick gap in the wind gusts that caused him to catch a glimpse of my red tail lights flashing below. He climbed down to help.

I was so thankful that this man had cared enough to look, to stop, and then come back to search, and that he was determined enough to keep searching until he found me. He was at the exact right place at exactly the right time, an incredibly kind Canadian who was willing to hear from God, and then watch out for me at the precise time and place where I needed help the most.

He agreed to take me to the nearest place where I could wait out the storm. This place was a small mom-and-pop-operated pub and small hotel with only four rooms. If there were no rooms, at least I could sit in the lobby and then call for a tow truck from the nearest town (over two hours behind me). The man assured me that most of the tow trucks had cranes that could lift vehicles, a necessity for the territory.

I gathered my purse and my dog, and got out of the Jeep. I realized I had failed to thank him or offer to pay him for his trouble, but when I turned, he was gone. To this day, I don't know whether he was an angel who just disappeared in the whiteout, or just a human being who took it upon himself to look after a complete stranger, driving through dangerous whiteout conditions to rescue me, my own personal human guardian angel. Either way, he was my provision, my "ever-present help in times of trouble" (Psalm 46:1).

[Valorie's challenges were far from over. The storm grew in intensity throughout the night, which she spent in a small room with her dog, a cot, toilet, and sink, with the winds damaging the roof and bringing down trees and branches all around them. Still, she was glad to be there instead of her car. The next morning she went with the tow truck to lift her car by crane from the ravine. She continues the morning of Day 3:]

They picked the car up and placed it on the side of the road, a maneuver they had clearly done many times before. Remarkably enough, the car started, and had no apparent damage—not even a scratch. Looking down at the place where the car had been, I was astounded that I was able to climb out of that ravine in a raging wind and blinding snow while carrying my dog and my purse, my guide a few steps ahead, leading me to each foothold, all the way up. It seemed to be a daunting climb, even in daylight with no blizzard-like conditions. God truly was "my strength and my shield" (Psalm 28:7).

Valorie made it to the dock just in time to catch the noon ferry, enduring twenty-five-foot waves and rough seas throughout most of the ten-hour journey across the strait. It took several more hours driving through blizzard-like conditions to make it to Newark, but in the end, she was able to enjoy the Macy's Thanksgiving Day Parade and a wonderful meal in New York City before making another full day's drive back to sunny Florida.

PART FIVE

THE FRUiT

Lowell: It's all about the people.

The long-term benefits of Young American Showcase will continue for generations to come, and on every possible level. The following stories capture some of the personal, spiritual, and professional growth, and allow a glimpse into lives changed through the Showcase ministry.

THE APPOINTMENTS

We mentioned that each school concert felt like a "divine appointment," the right message on just the right day, with people in the audience whose future depended on that perfect timing. The following account describes just such an appointment, demonstrating why God went to extraordinary lengths to get bands to the gig on time, and why the bands worked so hard once they got there to show love and energy to the students. This story also shows the ripple effect of their work—and of how God used those unlikely testimonies to change lives and save souls, sometimes in dramatic fashion.

ANGELS IN ALASKA – THE REST OF THE STORY

A few pages ago, Stan Arthur told a dramatic story, "Steep Grade Ahead," about God's protection on the road. This was not Stan's first "road rescue" experience. Previously, during a tour in Alaska, his band was headed across a long stretch of desolate territory to make an 8:30 a.m. show in Fairbanks. It took miraculous intervention, but the band made it to that school just in time to set up for the assembly. One troubled young teen at that performance came back to the night show, and what happened next served as a powerful reminder for years to come that, even in the most difficult circumstances, the mission was key, God was most definitely in it, and the method worked.

Remember, each band had a booker who made all the arrangements for shows, scheduling them down to the finest detail. Stan Arthur told his story about God's protection over his band on the road to Fairbanks, Alaska, at a Showcase reunion in 2007, and the booker who had arranged for the Fairbanks show, a fellow named Bob Miller, was there listening. Bob was a faithful friend who had been with the company almost from the very beginning of Showcase. After the reunion, Bob wrote a letter that perfectly illustrates why bands worked so hard to make every show the best it could be. Following is an excerpt from that letter (the full "Angels in Alaska" story and letter are in Diving into the Deep*):*

» Bob Miller:

Fairbanks had only two high schools, but after that show, one of them produced the strongest testimonial letter we ever received. It was penned by an eighteen-year-old young man approximately nine months after that most important evening concert, a concert made possible by the events on that overnight trip and, therefore, an indispensable miracle in God's plan that directly led to this young man's introduction to and acceptance of a personal relationship with Jesus. Both Fairbanks high schools were on an extremely tight schedule, and the morning assembly for that next morning had no room to be rescheduled. Had they missed that 8:30 a.m. show, one of those high schools, and this young man in particular, would have missed the opportunity entirely. The contents of that letter were heart-stopping.

The young man said that this particular Friday night was to be his first and last concert on this earth. Things were so bad in his life that he took the extraordinary step of putting only two and a half gallons of gas into his truck, carefully picking out the tree he planned to hit on his way home after the concert. Then he heard a sleep-starved young man, not much older than he was, tell him, not about religion, but about a relationship that was the most important thing in the lives of the group. The offer was made to talk to the students after the concert if they had any questions. Boy did he!

He wrote to us to let us know of the change that evening had made in his life. With his hope restored, he made plans for his future. The day he wrote us, he had just received his acceptance to the state teachers' university in Anchorage. His goal was to become a trained counselor, to help other high school kids. He just wanted us to know and to say, "thanks."

That letter was the first testimonial that every principal saw on my calls until our ministry finally came to an end. Sure, there were six to eight other letters from administrators and other young people right behind this one, but it was the only testimonial that almost every principal read to the very end.

Due to the real sacrifice of a faithful bunch of people, the intervention of the good Lord Himself, and the way-out thinking (literally) of a crazy booker, what a harvest God had in mind! It began with one desperate young guy who met his Master that night, and then continued with every school we were able to book because of his letter, which was largely responsible for the gospel being brought to thousands and thousands of other young people, many of whom were in circumstances similar to his. Who knows how many young people have found their own pathway to peace from that one soul?

Ron and Vi Lentini, two other wonderful people who had been in Showcase almost from the beginning as managers and several other roles, wrote Lowell a note that further proved the power of this radical experiment:

» Ron Lentini (1970-1985):

As manager, in school after school, I had kids come up to me, asking about the original guys they had seen three years before. Every kid remembered the show and especially the guys' testimony from the night show. Almost everyone had a story about how that night and that show had a major impact on their lives. That's when I realized that there would be several hundred thousand souls in Heaven as a result of this work.

Line of students waiting to get in to the night show

This example of a young person pulled back from the brink of suicide was not an isolated case. Students battling all sorts of issues filled every gymnasium, from bullying to drug addiction, to abuse, and beyond. In God's perfect timing, when those students were feeling most isolated and at their peak of hopelessness, God brought them hope, and a way through their pain, through the tireless work of the Showcase family.

» Monty Godfrey (1985-1988):

Impact in Detroit

During my first year on the road, we spent quite a bit of time in the Detroit area. We met a young man, which will remain nameless although I remember his name well. He was a junior in high school and had seen Free Fare the year before. He happened to be a bass player and a huge Duran Duran fan, so he and I had two things in common. He showed up at several of our other shows in the area, very eager to help wherever we needed, and had expressed interest in auditioning for Showcase during his senior year. He was a great guy and had an amazing attitude. I believe it was our last show in Detroit when he came up to the door of the truck and said he wanted something we had. What he wanted was a relationship with Christ, and we welcomed him into the truck as he accepted the Lord that night. I tried to keep in touch with him to some degree and told him I would let him know when and if another band would be up his way.

As things went, I was going to be in Detroit again the following year. I was excited to call him and tell him the news! I called his home number and his mother answered. Not long before that call, her son had been hit and killed by a bus as he was walking across a busy intersection. Shocked, I told her why I was calling. She recalled him having fond memories of spending time with us the year before. She thanked us for taking him in and befriending him as we had done. I have wondered ever since if she ever knew about the decision he made in our truck the year before. It did not occur to me to ask her. What I know is this: he made a decision that night, which secured him a place in Heaven. I am looking forward to seeing him again!

» Steve Tharp (1987-1991):

Worst Rookie in Showcase

My rookie year in The Edge had me performing back-to-back after shows with the amazingly humble vet, Dave Torguson, sharing the gospel. Derek Selby made us learn how to share the gospel quickly because he understood the mission; he also knew that Dave and I would share Jesus all night, if allowed. I have hundreds of stories that I could share from this band. The youth were often very open with us, because they knew we would be driving away to another city, and not telling anyone their stories or getting them in trouble. And, I was their age, so they could relate to me. I had no degree in counseling. However, the Holy Spirit was my counsel. I used to pray silently in my heart while the youth were sharing, that the Holy Spirit would give me the right words, and He always did.

I was most likely the worst rookie in the history of Showcase. However, because of great training and the grace of God, I may have been one of the most improved by the end of my first tour. When I was a rookie, we had quite a few "religious experiences," both good and bad. And, we broke bread together and remembered Jesus often, as they say.

[*The Edge* was a concept band out of Showcase that began in the late '80s and '90s. They used the same methods as Free Fare and Freedom Jam: day shows followed by a night show where they shared the gospel. The bands were aptly named, as the intention was to push the illusion farther toward the edge of seemingly outrageous rebellion they were seeing in the students coming to their concerts, to reach this new breed of student, and to adapt and change to the newer grain of music in that era.]

To succeed in your mission, adapt to your audience. Experiment. Push boundaries. Grow.

My second year, the rest of the band members were all rookies. I stood back-to-back with Tom Brown or Matt Grover night after night, sharing the gospel. Then Pat Flynn joined us. Pat came to Showcase as a homeless teenager. He slept on the floor of our hotel rooms the first few months of tour because he was not used to a bed. Pat had long hair on one side of his head and the other side was shaved. He, more than the others, realized the mission right away. So, although Pat didn't feel ready to share the gospel himself, he would send the heavy, dark, harder to reach youth that were drawn to him over to speak to me once he realized that they needed the peace and freedom found in a relationship with Jesus. So, Pat, the one that might have seemed too far over the edge, the homeless guy who slept in a graveyard that was close to the hotel the first week of tour, was there for the right reason, and for a purpose. I have many more stories about this version of The Edge with Tom Brown, Matt Grover, Stephen Dick, and Pat Flynn. We won "Band of the Year" in 1998, after having eight different managers during the tour. We were the band that could not make it down from western Canada to attend the closing end-of-the-year camp, because our truck would catch fire whenever we took our foot off the gas pedal to slow down or stop for more diesel. "Hey, your truck is on fire..." "Yeah we know. We're just trying to make it to the next mechanic, thanks!" I guess we had to have a lot of faith to drive that truck.

» Chris Lundquist (1983-1985):

Rescued - 2006
In 2006, a few Showcasers managed a small-scale "reboot" of Showcase, with two bands touring Kentucky, Tennessee, and the Carolinas. Lowell Lytle himself came out and helped get it off the ground. This time around, bullying was the big buzzword in schools, and our band, New Anthem, had a powerful anti-

bullying message in the day show, including the lead singer's personal story about his best friend, who died by suicide because of bullying. It was a gripping story that always made a positive impact, encouraging kids not to keep their struggle to themselves, but to open up and tell a friend, family, or teacher. The magnitude of this message hit us the first day of tour. In a typical Tennessee high school, the band did their day show, and came back the next night to do the night show concert where we would reiterate the anti-bullying message and present the gospel. Prior to the show, one boy approached the band and thanked us profusely for coming to their school. "You see," he said, "yesterday before you came, I was planning to commit suicide. I was actually going to take my life yesterday. Then I saw your concert, and you talked about suicide, and you said, 'Don't hold it in; let someone know what's going on, and they can help.' So I'm still here today, thanks to you. I decided not to kill myself because of what you said." And that was just the first day. Many similar stories unfolded regularly during the two years of the 2006–2008 reboot. It was awesome to be a part of such a meaningful and impactful experience, to be used by God in such a way again.

When your mission is your driving force, when you empty yourself daily for people with the one goal of illuminating Jesus to them, seeing that work bear fruit is incredibly rewarding—and also creates an indelible bond. You care about "what happens next." Even though there was a process for follow-up handled by home office, sometimes a band would take it upon themselves to stay connected in a way that would allow them to continue to encourage students touched by their message. The 1989–1990 McVey Freedom Jam came up with a newsletter to do just that.

» Jeff Siebert (1989-1991):

Sharing this memory and praising the efforts that many of us made to share God's Word. We created these monthly newsletters and mailed them to new Christians as a way to keep them connected, encouraged and to continue watering the seeds that were planted.

Hello there!
    We just thought that we would drop you a line to let you know that we're still thinking about you and praying for you. We've all put together a verse that means something to us and an explanation to go along with it. We encourage you to look up these verses and take them to heart.

                            God bless you, -Freedom Jam

    Jeff Siebert - Proverbs 3:5-6 One of the greatest things about being a Christian is putting your faith in God. When we listen to our heart, God can talk to us more easily. The more you get to know him, the easier it is to see where he wants you to go. So when you pray, let God come into your heart, and ask him to lead the way for you.

    Kirk Engel - Philippians 1:6 Letting God be God: Faith is the assumption that God is as good as his word. So when you're not sure on some things, you've just got to have trust & faith in the bible.

    Dave McVey - Philippians 4:6 I challenge you as a new Christian to trust God with everything in your life. The Bible says not to worry about anything, but to pray about everything. With this you will recieve a peace inside, that no one can take away.

    Ed Pittman - Psalm 23:4 When we find ourselves at the lowest points in our life, (the valley) God tells us to have complete trust in him and to fear nothing, for he will be with us always.

    Rich Varno - Matthew 6:14-15 I used to be very big on holding grudges. Because of this I carried a lot of anger around inside of me. Now when you have all of this pent up anger inside of you, life becomes very unpleasant. I urge you to use this verse to gain peace with yourself through Jesus.

    Pete Janett - John 13:4-5 This verse shows how Jesus took the role of a slave to teach his Disiples a lesson in humility; serve others, not yourself! That's how this band gets along and survives. We'll be keeping you in our prayers.

    D-Love - John 3:16 This verse tells how God loves us so much that he sent his only son down to Earth to die for us so that we could gain eternal life. When you accepted Jesus your life was changed forever. The prayer that you prayed that night was the greatest thing you could have done! I pray that you will continue reading your Bible and that you will always keep your eyes on Jesus!

GROWING UP SHOWCASE

*Lowell: Don't doubt in the darkness what God
reveals to you in the light.*

Many Showcase members shared their gratitude for the personal, spiritual, and professional growth that came out of their time with Showcase. Their recollections remind us that these were young men, not professional counselors, not seasoned evangelists. They learned to be in the moment, to listen and respond the best they could to young people struggling with life, and to trust that God would give them the words to say. They were trained on the front lines, several times a day, almost every day, and quickly got over their fear and doubt:

» Lance Abair (1972-1983):

Road Test

I often went out on the road to evaluate bands, but the first time, Lowell came along to teach me about the difficult job of critiquing. The first show was in Springville, Utah. I remember Lowell and I were sitting up in the balcony bleachers of a gym with the band playing on the floor. It was not anywhere close to the level of showmanship that I expected. It was rough. I freaked and asked Lowell if I could leave. I had to get out of there. Lowell said, "No. I want you to see and feel the pain of the performance greenery." I stayed and finished watching the show. I needed to shift gears in order to meet these guys where they were and try to impart what I knew they needed to do to improve. Doing this was very satisfying to me. Building into people is a gratifying thing to do and I enjoy it. I actually enjoyed all eleven years of it.

I remember all those guys working through unbelievable schedules, weather, and fiascos. I have a great respect for those who weathered the storm of touring and came out on the other side with maturity, motivation, leadership skill, unfaltering responsibility, and many other strengths. I thought of Showcase as a company of musical marines. It was not all about being a great musician, although I was really into promoting that too. It was the process of growing up, of meeting test after test, that turned these young guys into solid men. Respect.

It is a delicate dance to go into a public school and communicate the gospel. I think Lowell had it right. Our bands went to each school and, based upon their performance and communication they "won the right" to speak. No Bible thumping, no fire and brimstone. Just meet the kids where they are and communicate the four spiritual laws in a casual and friendly manner. After being there for eleven years, I saw the results, and they were strong.

A word from the editors: You may be reading this and find yourself confused about "gospel conversations," a "relationship with Christ, "accepting Jesus," and other Christian-faith-related jargon. So many of us have spent years in church and know a lot about the story of Jesus, but don't really know Jesus personally, have never felt Him close to us, have never heard His voice—so these conversations are a mystery. Just keep reading.

More now on the incredible personal development, mentoring, and spiritual growth that took place every day.

» Ralph Watkins (1980–1985):

Groundhog Day

Occasionally, you would hear about some guy, some band member, that couldn't take it. The band would wake up in the morning and the guy would be gone. Right in the middle of the tour bookings and all, he would just walk away from it. I certainly was not going to let that happen to me. Thankfully, that did not happen in our group. But there were a lot of conflicts in our group. So how do you resolve that? You just sit down face-to-face and say, okay, what is the issue, what can we do, how can we help you get through this?

All of this adds up to a tremendous opportunity for personal development. There is just no end. It's like the movie *Groundhog Day*. Every day you wake up, it's the same day. It was like that, every freaking day! You get up, go eat breakfast, you go and play shows, get some lunch, then do an afternoon show. You get dinner, do the night show, tear down, go back to the motel and crash, and do this over and over and over and over. But, you're presented with another opportunity every day to get it right. Something didn't go well? What happened? What didn't work right? What should we learn from that, that we could apply the next day to do a better job of making it happen?

So, it's an endless pursuit. You wake up the next morning and do it all over again. We messed up yesterday? No problem. It is literally a new day, and we are doing the same identical thing and we can work through that problem. Honestly, toward the end of the tour it became an endurance test. You tell yourselves and eachother, "We have another two weeks before the end of the tour. I know we can do this." That little groundhog, by the end of the movie *Groundhog Day*, stayed there all day until he got it right. We had that same opportunity on the road.

» Roger Blackington (1970-1971):
I saw kids in Florida, especially Okeechobee, who really responded to the gospel message. I remember a girl there just breaking down as she received Christ that night! I saw the impact of the school show and the difference with the production at night, and "winning the right to be heard" in action.

» Lang Bliss (1978-1984):
I was a new believer but the first person I witnessed to was a stage crew guy at a school in Canada, and he accepted Jesus at the night show. It was exciting to see that happen! My first year on the road, I gave the appeal in the night show.

» Chris Bouvier (1983-1985):
I personally spoke with a teenage boy who talked of suicide, saying that he didn't feel like he could talk to his parents or teachers about problems, so I asked him to go to church and ask a preacher if he could listen to him once a week…and I told him that he could chat as if they were best friends. I asked him to do so immediately so I could ask him about his experience at our night show several days later. He did. He said he never felt more relief in his life, so I asked him to talk to the preacher about becoming friends with Jesus Christ so he would have someone to ask for guidance all the time. He assured me he would. I noticed a calm sense of demeanor that night in that young man.

» Joe Brown (1969-1972):
For Lowell Lytle, the Young American Showcase mission was about spreading the gospel. Some kids responded positively to that message. Others just enjoyed listening to the band, had fun at our shows, and wanted to talk with us. A few followed the band to shows at other schools and became real fans. So, sharing the gospel was the stated mission, and to a certain extent Lowell's desired goal was fulfilled. Many kids indicated they had prayed with us and accepted Christ as their personal Savior. Who knows how many of those planted seeds sprouted? Who knows what effects still ripple through the lives and families of those kids who heard Free Fare, Freedom Jam, or any of the other groups? Only Heaven knows. I think all YAS veterans hope someday to find out just how many lives we touched. Perhaps in the next world, someone will approach each of us and say, "I want to thank you for what you did when you came to our school. It changed my life forever. I am here because of what you did."

» Steve Soderquist (1983-1985):

I spent a lot of time in personal reflection and, at first, I felt I was simply going through the motions. Later in life, I started to understand the monumental impact the YAS experience had, not only on my life, but also in how my life had reached others, fellow band members and audiences. The smallest pebble creates ripples that can be felt around the world.

» Alec Johannson:

One of the best things that happened to me is that I opened an email around 2010, a few years after my time with Showcase. A person who had seen the Smith Freedom Jam in Minnesota sent me a message a few years earlier, but I had not checked that email account for years because I had changed to a different server. As I read the letter, I remembered speaking with him after the show at his school. He purchased both posters and we spoke for a bit during load out. He wanted to receive Christ into his life. I told him about a book called *How to be a Christian without Being Religious*. (Lance recommended this book to me and it really helped prepare me to come to Showcase.) We wrote a few letters back and forth for a couple of months, and then I lost contact with him. In his email to me, he stated that, because of Freedom Jam and our night show testimony, and his conversations with me, he asked Jesus Christ to be his personal Lord and Savior. In the years to follow, he became a strong Christ follower. He met a very nice Christian girl and got married. He then mentioned that, because of all of this, he became a minister and, soon after, his wife and he were able to get their own church, which they both operate to this day, somewhere in Minnesota. I have always said that if this student was the only reason for my existence, he was a very good one. The fact that a small seed grew into a church, was used to spread the gospel of Jesus, was shared with others by this man and his wife, affirmed for me that I used my time here wisely.

» Paul Turner (1976-1978):

I saw MANY seeds planted in the lives of stage crews and students who attended night shows to hear the gospel shared among many surprised concertgoers. I understood very well (still do) that the moments of the night rap and our interaction with the students after each show were much more important than all the music we played.

Since "graduating" from Showcase, Paul has written hundreds of songs, served in music and youth ministry, and produced music projects designed to help people have gospel conversations through the vehicle of music. He recently wrote and recorded a song for this project. Following are the lyrics:

God's Rock and Roll Army[3]
I put my life on hold many years ago
For a chance to see the world through rock and roll
To experience so many things, and so many miles
An opportunity to watch myself grow (and be...)

Chorus: Part of God's Rock and Roll Army
Singing songs and spreading truth throughout the land
We came from far and wide serving side by side for His glory
And His message made us more than just a band.

How did a band of strangers become a band of brothers?
And why did they work so hard to earn the right
To bring God's truth to those who needed to hear it?
Where did they get the desire and strength to fight? (We were...)

Chorus: Part of God's Rock and Roll Army
Singing songs and spreading truth throughout the land
We came from far and wide serving side by side for His glory
And His message made us more than just a band.

Bridge:
What began as one man's vision grew to become what we all shared
Like an army we headed into battle
where every soldier knew to be faithful and true
Because we knew that ears were listening, so what are they gonna hear?
And we knew that eyes were watching. We had to make it clear
That Jesus is the leader of our band! (We were...)

Chorus: Part of God's Rock and Roll Army
Singing songs and spreading truth throughout the land
We came from far and wide to serving by side for His glory
And He still uses us and the seeds we sow,
And we're thankful for the chance to rock and roll!

---

[3]This song is the soundtrack to the book trailer for God's Rock and Roll Army, found on the Encourage Publishing YouTube channel.

CARRY ON, MY WAYWARD SON

Lowell: I will win and you will lose.

One of the biggest lessons these young road warriors had to learn was "It's not about you, so carry your weight." In short, this mission was too important to coddle under-performers, or allow anyone to get stuck in the trap of focusing exclusively on their own strengths—or weaknesses. In addition, with only four or five band members, all functioning at their maximum, if you do not hold your weight, no one else can help. Everyone was expected to step up, improve, be their best, give their all, and function together as a well-oiled machine. Repeatedly, musicians would perform while they were sick or injured, with broken equipment or in dangerous circumstances. They would overcome everything to earn the right to be heard, making sure they did not miss their opportunity at the end to share their faith. Those few that buckled, rebelled, or just did not care could expect a visit if their manager could not get through—sometimes from Lowell himself. They would usually be given an opportunity to make a correction, but would be excused from the group if they did not respond. Several veterans had stories about lessons learned on the road, and many of them involved setting aside their insecurities and egos, and learning how to put forth extraordinary effort to do their part.

» Michael (Jonesy) Jones (1980-1982):

"Turn it around or you are gone."

I would like to begin by thanking Mr. Lytle for recognizing and unearthing my potential as an entertainer and a man. I was quite the diamond in the rough. I think the majority of the staff either did not see my potential, or thought mining it would take too much effort and time and the yield may not be worth it. Mr. Lytle made me his personal project.

I had sung in a lot of choirs and in a church singing group that traveled regionally, but nothing like this. I remember in my audition, a guy by the name of Mark Lach asked me if I knew the difference between the sound of a kick drum and a snare. I didn't. I'm sure this is where I lost a lot of the staff's confidence. Mark was wonderful explaining this simple concept to me and how it could be the basis for making music visual. I think this grace afforded to me was to see if I was coachable.

I was placed in a band with two front men, Chip Daignault, and me. Chip was a veteran front man, a dancer/acrobat. He was everything I was not. Somehow I survived camp (barely). Every band left camp with a staff person to get them acclimated to the road. Our band got the president of the company, Mr. Lytle. We played three shows a day, and after every show, we would have a critiquing session, usually over a meal. After about a week, the critiquing sessions changed. My band would be at one table eating and laughing, and at another table, Mr. Lytle and I would be working on my performance—or lack thereof. He would start each of our personal critiquing sessions by saying, "Mike, I like you; you have qualities that I want for myself. I'd like to meet your parents. You're a leader; the Lord has built you to lead, given you stature and presence that make people want to follow you." Then he would go off on me about how bad I was doing in the show. After a few days of this, I thought I would help him get started. So, I'd say, "You like me. I've got qualities you want for yourself; you'd like to meet my parents. I'm a leader. God's hooked me up. Okay, let's begin."

It was so much to work on; I was overwhelmed. It got to the point that if Mr. Lytle was in the audience, I was bound to mess up. When you are mining potential, sometimes it gets dirty. Mr. Lytle wasn't afraid to use dynamite. He went around to each of my bandmates individually and asked them, "Who do you think is the weak link of your band?" Of course, they said I was; and that was the truth. Next, in a meeting with all of us, he announced that all of my bandmates said I'm holding the band back. I knew it was true. He presented it as if my brothers had turned on me. For a moment I was crazy mad, hurt, and disappointed at my bros.

He told me one day that he had spoken to his youngest daughter, Laura. She had asked him to come home and carve a pumpkin with her for Halloween. He told her he couldn't because Mike Jones wouldn't let him. Then he pointed his boney finger at me and said, "I won't let you rob Laura and me of our time together. I'm going home to carve that pumpkin." Then he showed me a plane ticket with my name on it, to my home airport for a week later. "I'm leaving you with Stan Arthur. Turn it around or you are gone."

Each show I was trying to fix everything—I had about sixty notes per show of things to correct. I finally realized that I needed to eat this elephant one bite at a time. I would concentrate on five to ten notes a show. It took weeks to whittle down that long list, but daily improvement turned down the heat on the "send Jonesy home" stuff.

Probably the most difficult part of my role was the inspirational speech, which I had to learn word for word. It was hard for me to deliver it in a believable way. So, I had to make it mine—my words with my delivery.

A couple of months later, we are doing a show, and in the audience were Lowell and Barbara Lytle. They had come unannounced. My bandmates were hoping I didn't notice for fear I may fall apart, as Mr. Lytle had been my kryptonite. I saw them and did my thing. We had a great show. Afterward, I went backstage and passed out for a few minutes. I had given it my all; now it was time to face the critique.

He had only words of praise and was so impressed with my speech, that he had recorded it and had it sent to the other seven bands to learn word for word, with all the inflections. I still had lots to learn, but I was on my way.

I have heard it said that you will always be loyal to the place where you find your identity. That is Showcase for me. I wish and hope that my son will find a place and a people that will help him unearth his potential.

In closing, Mr. Lytle, I like you. You have qualities that I want for myself. I wish I could have met your parents. You surely are a great leader; the Lord has built you to lead, given you stature and presence that make people want to follow you. Once again, thank you.

» Don Morrissette (1972-1975):

Thank you for not firing me!

Following is a humorous anecdote, an incident that occurred during one of our night concerts, with my brother band members Mark Walker, Dave Sheirman, and Bobby King. Bobby, Dave, and Mark had just completed the "Pencils Skit." Then, Bobby sat down center stage with his acoustic guitar to sing the song "If" by the band Bread, preparing to deliver the "rap" afterward. Suddenly, people from the audience began throwing pennies at him. A few coins were thrown very hard, some even hitting Bobby and his guitar. I got so angry I was seeing red! I grabbed my microphone and began yelling at the audience to stop it! I said something to the effect of, "Quit it! You people should all be ashamed of yourselves! Bobby is trying to sing a song for you, and you are deliberately trying to hurt him!" At that point, everyone stopped throwing the coins and, immediately, it got so quiet that one could hear the proverbial pin drop! Bobby then said to me, into his mic, in a very calm voice, "It's okay Donnie. Don't worry, it's cool." So Bobby sang the song, gave the rap, and we ended the show.

After the show, when the four of us went to the front of the stage to sign the usual autographs, to my incredulous surprise, each person for whom I signed my autograph told me how deeply sorry they were about what they had done. I felt like a heel! While breaking down the equipment at the end of the night, Mark Walker came to me and said, "Don, I think you might be in a little bit of trouble. You see, sitting in the audience tonight were Lowell, Lance, Barbara, and Donn Kenyon!" *[At that time, Donn Kenyon was the spiritual director.]* When he told me that, I got so scared I almost passed out... literally! During the entire drive back to our rooms, I was shaking like a leaf. I was certain that Lowell would send me home!

When we finally arrived at the rooms, Steve Hornyak came in and told me to follow him. As we walked into his room, right there, waiting for me were Lowell, Lance, Barb, and Donn Kenyon. I felt as though I was going to drop dead, right then and there! However, Lowell, with his deep, soothing, Lurch-like voice, calmly told me to sit down. He then proceeded to tell me that he knew exactly how I had felt when I lost my cool, as he had done the same thing once before, during one of his performances! He explained to me that the throwing of pennies at Bobby was only the audience's way of trying to get into the "Pencils Skit." They just wanted to be part of the show, and this was merely their way of expressing it. Needless to say, I was never so relieved in my eighteen years of living! I thanked him for not firing me, and for rationally explaining to me a lesson that I took away with me for the rest of my life to date. Lowell, dear friend and brother, I would like to take this opportunity to, once again, thank you for all the help that you gave me, and for teaching me a very valuable lesson.

Lowell, as president of the company, set the highest of standards, both for performance and for conduct, and made sure everyone knew and understood what was expected, and what was at stake. His presence commanded respect. Everyone wanted to please him, to meet his expectations. He could have chosen to play the role of a tyrant, cold, aloof, and unforgiving. Yet, like a loving father, he saw the individuals in the bands as young men who would grow and learn; he knew their value, and gave their managers the support they needed to shape them into a tight-knit, effective band of brothers. In the previous story, Don was only eighteen, the same age as some of the students in the audience. In Jonesy's account, Lowell refused to give up on him and, thankfully, Jonesy never gave up, either. Lowell certainly had a way with words when trying to get the attention of a band member in need of some coaching:

» Brent Woody (1976-1990):

"You look like you might be dead."

It's the fall of 1976. I am a rookie in a Freedom Jam band made up of mostly all-star veterans. Tim Brownell, Mark Lach, Ronnie Hickman, Alec Johansson...and I believe the drummer was Dave "Yardbird" Yarborough. I think I'm keeping up with the vets fairly well. Lowell comes out to critique, and, honestly, I'm excited for him to see how well I'm doing in the midst of these seasoned entertainers. So, it's Lowell's first time critiquing our show, the first of two back-to-back shows in the morning. We're playing in an auditorium with a backstage dressing room. We do the show, kids go wild, and we gather in the dressing room to hear Lowell's critique. He starts going through the band, one by one.

"Mark, man, you are the consummate front man, always engaging the kids, all over the stage. There's nothing I can say to make you better. Just the best we've ever had. Tim, you are the best comedian in the company ever. Your sense of what's funny, your timing, all perfect. Ronnie, what a singer! You are warm on stage, always communicating, and funny. Alec, what an asset you are to the company and this band. You're just a great bass player with incredible energy, always smiling, great one-to-one communication. Fantastic."

He gets to me, and I'm excited about what's coming. "Brent…[long hesitation] You looked like the six-dollar man on that stage. In fact, you look like you might be dead. Maybe we should prop you up like a dead body and introduce you as a corpse or a cardboard cutout. I don't even know what to tell you to do—it would be like rebuilding a personality."

Well, that was not quite what I was expecting, but I took it in good stride, and did my best to improve. I was never a great entertainer like my bandmates, but it sure made for a good story!

Brent, in his usual humility, does not give himself credit. He did indeed improve, and later Lowell saw his leadership strengths and tapped him to work in the home office. Since that time, Brent remained in the business of changing lives, graduating from law school and becoming a successful attorney. In 2012, Brent founded the Justice Restoration Center (Dunedin, Florida), working to rescue, represent, and restore victims and survivors of human trafficking, change laws, and advise others around the world on issues of human trafficking.

Your people are your most valuable asset.

What about the inevitable conflicts that would arise between band members? The following story by one of the Showcase managers illustrates the importance of unity and cohesiveness within each group—and the power of prayer:

»Tom Miller (1975-1985):

The first half of the '76-'77 tour had come and gone normally, and we all headed home for Christmas break. In January, the Blizzard of 1977 hit with a vengeance, and school closings took three of our bands, including mine, off the road, with no indication of how long schools would be closed. So, we all headed back to Florida to regroup.

Bookers had scrambled to put together enough shows in the South for two of the three groups to get back on the road. As it worked out, three from my Free Fare (Bil Curry, Gary Kolosey, Paul Turner) and three from another Free Fare (Rich Thomas, David Hayes, Marty Resch) were combined into a Freedom Jam show and quickly worked up the new set during a mini-rehearsal camp. We hit the road after a quick couple of shows in Florida to tune things up.

A few weeks into tour, the show was coming together and the guys were adjusting to the new lineup, but there was some tension here and there, as if they were still two three-piece bands on stage who happened to be playing with each other. Six great guys, six good attitudes, but something just wasn't right.

Somewhere in Alabama, the tension spilled over, and there had been some very stressful times. The guys were able to set that aside during the shows, but in the van, in the locker rooms and most anywhere outside of show time, the tension had been getting worse. We had been staying in some apartment-style accommodations for a week or so but were getting ready to move again. It was Easter morning and my wife, Linda, and I had the group get together in one of the rooms for a meeting; we thought it might be nice to have communion together, so we brought supplies for that. Before we had our closing prayer time leading into communion, we read Matthew 5:23-24:

> "Therefore, if you are offering your gift at the altar and there remember that your brother or sister has something against you, leave your gift there in front of the altar. First go and be reconciled to them; then come and offer your gift (NIV)."

I commented that we should clear the air between us if we were going to have communion together. We all bowed heads, and it was silent for a while... kind of a long while. I think it was Bil who first let out a little sigh and then started out with a heartfelt prayer involving a desire for unity and brotherhood. From there, the prayers worked their way all around the room—Rich, Gary, David, Paul, Marty, Linda and me. It was electric. I choke up some even now, just remembering the strong shift in mood and the strong sense of relief every one of us was feeling.

It was like someone threw a breaker and the power came on. The show went from "decent" to downright awesome! The rides to and from shows, the meals together, the locker room banter, rehearsal time—everything was different. The boys truly were in sync. These guys became so tight as a group and were having so much fun together on-stage and off; a giant weight had been lifted. Our audiences, both day show and night show, were totally with us from the very first note until we drove away. It was powerful.

Not too long after that, Lowell and Lance popped up at an assembly show on their way to see another group. The boys did their thing. After the show, Lowell asked me to get the group together before we moved on. I remember all of us sitting on a grassy berm on the edge of the parking lot. Lowell looked over at Lance and said, "You start."

Lance looked around at each of the guys, then said, "That wasn't a show... that was an ONSLAUGHT!" Then he let out with one of those classic "Lance" laughs! I'll never forget those words, and I'll bet the guys never forgot, either.

After a little light critiquing and catching up, off they went to another group and off we went to our next school.

From that moment on, there was no question about it—whatever school we pulled in to, we knew we were going to blow them away. Watching these guys relate to the kids off-stage as effectively as they did on-stage was just so rewarding. We became known as the "Supergroup," and had an absolute blast together. We played the NAMM show in Atlanta, even got back together again for a week to play a special festival event in New Bedford, Massachusetts, that summer. In anyone's book, Miller Freedom Jam I turned out to be a uniquely special group.

Most rookies were young—still teenagers themselves with more raging hormones than common sense—and came in either with a healthy case of ego or crushing insecurities—or both. Few had traveled; none under such demanding conditions. The importance of putting the mission before your own ego and insecurities was expected equally from everyone—even the president's son. Imagine being a child of the man whom everyone was simultaneously afraid of and grateful to for the opportunity of a lifetime. You grow up in Showcase under the shadow of his gigantic presence, and though you are deeply loved and cherished by the man, you know you have to prove yourself. Like everyone else, you have to earn your right to be heard, your place in the group, and you finally get your shot.

» David Lytle (1978-1990):

Most Improved Rookie

In the fall of 1980, in the first month of my first tour, I had the task of mixing the sound of the Resch Free Fare, a vet-heavy band that was premiering and fine-tuning an all-new day show skit based on TV reruns of the '60s and '70s. Of course, I wanted to do my best, pull my weight, and impress all around me: students, teachers, my band members, and visiting Showcase staff.

After all, I was the president's son and I definitely felt the need to "represent." And, naturally, I wanted very desperately to believe in myself. However, at this point in my life I was carrying the usual youthful bundle of insecurities that could be expected to reside within a melancholic kid raised in the shadow of the "Super Daddy."

Simply put, I did not allow myself the privilege of believing that I was any good at my job. I wanted to believe, but to believe for one moment was to position myself for an ego-crushing fall. Better to go on believing in my never-fading mediocrity than to believe in my own competence for one moment, only to be thrown to the ground by the least criticism of the lowest denominator.

THE FRUIT

My father, Lowell, had met up with us to fine-tune the new skit and generally impose his artistic touches on the show. It was after one particularly fine day show while I was packing equipment and cords when a student, who had hung back from returning to class, strolled up to me and said, "You did a great job of mixing sound today. Very well balanced."

Instead of thanking him graciously, I shook my lowered head and with eyes averted I said, "No, I didn't. I did a crap job." and then proceeded to offer specifics on how I had failed.

He just looked down at the same floor that I had been staring at, turned away, and walked off.

I was startled out of my lovely depression when Mr. Lytle suddenly and sharply called me over.

He got up in my face, like Sargent Carter did with Gomer Pyle, and said with utter finality, "Don't you ever contradict anyone giving you a compliment. It doesn't matter if they're wrong. You may suck to high heaven. But...you...look them in the eye, smile, and say thank you. And you make them believe it. That kid gave you the gift of a compliment and you spat on it. You don't have the right to make him feel like a fool for giving you that gift." Pause. "Did you think for one moment about what you were really saying to him? Do you realize that by saying that you sucked you were actually telling him that *his* opinion sucked? Who do you think you are?"

My dad didn't give me the Sunday school lecture about treating others as we would like to be treated. He didn't have to. I already knew the Golden Rule of "Do unto others as you would have others do unto you." I had been living it most of my life, but it wasn't until that moment that I realized I had only been focused on my half of the equation. I had been giving, all right, but only when I was in a state of emotional surplus; I had not learned how to take my eyes off myself and see other people's needs first, even when I was operating out of a deficit. I had never before noticed my failure to live up to Christ's example whenever I was sitting comfortably in my insecurities and the sick luxury of self-loathing. How did my low opinion of my mixing skills stack up to Jesus' prayers as He sweat blood? Thanks be to God that Christ was able to think of someone other than Himself when He was having a bad day.

Put most simply, I found myself empathizing with the kid that I had sent packing, having fully educated him concerning his inadequate evaluation of my performance. I earnestly wished that I could undo my selfish, ignorant, pointless crime. That could not be done. The kid was gone and I couldn't recognize him in a line-up because I had been studying my shoes instead of honoring him with a glance. However, by the grace of our God, I changed that day; not because the president of Young American Showcase had lectured me, and not because I had failed to earn his respect, but because I had the revelation that the other guy matters, more than my perception of me.

David most certainly did improve, and matured dramatically in self-esteem, confidence, and empathy that year. His 180-degree turnaround changed everything for him and for his teammates. He became a source of tremendous encouragement for his band of brothers, and completed his mission so strongly he was presented with the coveted "Rookie of the Year" award at the end of tour. "Growing up Showcase" certainly had its challenges, but it had its benefits too. Lowell and Barb began Showcase with three young children at their feet, and Connie, we learned, was an invaluable help in caring for them, all while she was growing up herself. Raising your children in such an environment meant time away, unstable schedules, and exposure to a constant parade of new and different experiences and people. Some would say that was not the most responsible way to raise a child, but the children themselves, now grown, did not see it that way at all. There were other children about, as well, from several of the other leaders' families. David's sister Debbie also worked in the home office and corresponded with some of the students who would write in. She could see the impact this ministry had and was able to follow up with those that needed some extra attention. The Lytles' youngest, Laura, gives us a window into her Showcase life.

» Laura (Lytle) Smith:

Growing up in Showcase to me was a normal life. I never knew anything different. I was two years old when Showcase began. It wasn't until much later in life that I realized it was not the norm to spend summers at rehearsal camp surrounded by young musical performers. When I was young, I spent most of my summer days swimming in the pool, playing with other kids, usually the children of band managers, or office personnel. My brother, David, and sister, Debbie, were usually put in charge of watching me during camp when my mom was training the managers about the financial responsibilities, or when she was preparing all of the meals for the whole camp.

As I got older, friends Mindi Abair, Vonnie Lentini, Kristen Hardley, Maria Brockus, all Showcase children, and sometimes my cousins, Jeff, Joe, and Jackie, would be there to swim, play games, and jump from one practice room to another to watch the bands. We girls would always choose one or two guys every year to be our secret crush. We all hoped to be chosen when they were practicing the "sing to the girl" song. The singer would come out to the audience and pull us up on stage to practice singing to a girl, and in the beginning, the guys were always very nervous. They would be sweating and shaking pretty badly, especially when they were singing to one of the adult office girls.

Some of my fondest memories were when I was allowed to join my dad out on the road and go from show to show at different schools. That is when I started to realize this was not a conventional life for a family. The Showcase musicians were friends of mine, and what I saw as "normal" was seen as completely different by the students. My friends were on stage performing the songs that we heard every day on the radio, but these students, girls and guys, would go crazy, screaming and crying at the concerts as if they were seeing the Beatles. After the show was over, I would help a couple band members sell posters and records. Once the students saw that I was with the band, they would ask me all kinds of questions about the band members. I got to see first-hand how the ministry worked. The students were amazed at how these rock and rollers could possibly have a relationship with the Lord and still be so cool.

By the time I was in high school, I spent part of the summer working in the office with data input and helping to make and purchase props for the skits. I was sent to the airport to pick up new musicians, as well as the vets. One time I was supposed to pick up a guy named Orlando. I waited in baggage claim for thirty minutes after the flight landed, but there wasn't anyone that looked like they needed a ride—except for one guy sitting in the corner wearing a multi-colored clown wig. I could not imagine that being the guy for camp. I got on the phone to have Orlando paged and, low and behold, that was the guy. He said he thought Brent Woody, one of the talent coordinators, would be picking him up; he was so embarrassed that a girl picked him up while he was wearing a clown wig! My life growing up was anything but normal, and I thank the Lord for it.

» Mindi Abair:

It's a Family Affair

[Like David Lytle and his sisters, Debbie and Laura, Lance and Linda Abair's daughter Mindi Abair grew up in Showcase. Mindi is an internationally recognized saxophonist, twice Grammy-nominated, and a widely respected leader in the music industry, serving as National Trustee for the National Academy of Recording Arts and Sciences. Everything she observed as a child became a huge part of her success later in life. She observes here the powerful long-term effects of the "love and energy" poured into the teams, through mentoring, strong leadership, consistent standards, and a common mission.]

While everyone coming through Showcase was eighteen or older, I got the incredible gift of experiencing that love, professionalism, and excellence taught and maintained throughout my childhood. That's what I call a great education.

Showcase was a huge force in shaping who I have become as an adult. I was the little kid running around, a fan of the music, of the new musicians coming in every year, and I sat in practice rooms for hours every day watching Free Fare and Freedom Jam bands rehearse, rock out, make mistakes, and even get critiqued by my dad or Lowell.

I was so young, I wasn't thinking what an impact all of these adventures could have on me. They were just that—adventures. Laura, Debbie, and I would spend our summer vacations together, hanging out with the bands at summer camp. When I've tried to explain what our "summer camp" looked and sounded like, I've come across blank stares of disbelief. It does sound outrageous, yet that was our "normal."

I took some lessons away that were invaluable. The one thing that was preached every day and in every way was excellence. Lowell and my father were constantly striving for excellence with the guys' musicianship, look, demeanor, showmanship, and spirit. "This is not a dress rehearsal. This is the BIG TIME!" I still hear Lowell's booming voice projecting that to every new crop of bands. I live my life by those words today. They cared about every detail so much, from sending the guys to get clothes at Michael and Toni's place to getting them cool haircuts, to working with their movements and interactions on stage. In my father's presentation on TP, or being "Totally Pro," he talked about everything from wearing cologne, to creating your own look—in other words, not looking like one of the people in the local mall you're walking through—and how to carry yourself properly in all situations. Who thinks of that stuff?

Other lasting gifts are the relationships and family that emerged. I know someone from Showcase in almost every city I play in. Guys call my dad and vice versa still today, from bonds they made thirty to forty years ago with him. He still keeps in touch. He still cares. In fact, we all care about each other and share this bond that is hard to describe. It's a true family. We were all a part of something so special; it continues to be a source of family and respect and camaraderie all these years later for everyone I've ever known who's gone through the Showcase experience in any role.

Lastly, what an amazing gift to know that my dad has been an incredible father figure to not just me, but hundreds of Showcase guys through many years. He has given so much of himself, and I know he's loved every minute of it. That's who he is. I've watched him give a sense of self-worth and confidence to so many that were at a formative stage in their lives. I've always thought he was the coolest dad in the world… that's just one of the many reasons.

PART SIX

ROAD WARRIORS

Lowell: You can't claim that you've been to a new state unless you go into a convenience store and buy a candy bar.

We have been covering a lot of heavy topics and stories, but there was a lot of laughter out on the road. Sometimes you just have to stop and appreciate the crazy, unpredictable incidents that happened in every band, on every tour, every year, as well as the antics any group of young men might pull to keep their sanity, or just have a good, stress-relieving laugh. What was it like on the road?

Aaron Stillings (1975–1977)

» Steve Soderquist (1983–1985):

The Directive

If anything can be said about being a part of Young American Showcase, having a lack of stories to tell for years, or even decades later, definitely isn't one of them. Every day brought something new, despite how many of us felt sometimes like it was a daily grind. Sure, there were certain aspects that seemed carbon-copied and rolled from one day to the next—new hotel, looks like the last hotel; new school, the only differences being the question of whether we were setting up in a gym, auditorium, or cafeteria. After that, nothing was as simple as day-to-day wash/rinse/repeat. We were musicians on the road with a message, and how we got to that message was at times so memorable they will stick with us forever.

It's the experiences that we all shared while performing that, many times, brought out the most unique memories: the makeshift drum riser collapsing due to the locks on the cafeteria tables not being secured at the Y-joints, or blown tweeters, or guitars popping strings, certainly all of us falling at some point on stage, or slipping, or missing a cue, not to mention the myriad times my fingers hit a bad note on the keyboard, or I just completely spaced out on what the next note even was.

Still, the directive was as old as time itself, passed down from generation to generation of performers of all kinds, no matter the venue or act: "The show must go on!"

Any performer worth their salt has had to experience something applicable to this motto. With the amount of shows we did, this was a daily challenge. Sure, there were plenty of times in the middle of a song, with our heads thrashing and rocking it out, that our thoughts were elsewhere. We'd be thinking, "I wonder if we're going to hit that Golden Corral we passed on the way here for dinner." Still, there were plenty of other moments when an all-you-can-eat buffet was the *last* thing on our minds.

» Wes Turner (1972–1973):

Boys Locker Room

[After arriving at a school, after student roadies had helped them set up, before students began filing in, the band would head to the boys' locker room to dress, and to prepare mentally and spiritually for the show. Wes Turner gives a colorful description of the scene.]

The air in the room hung heavy with the fragrance of Aqua-Net. From the wall of locked baskets guarding our privacy from young eyes, pungent odor tentacles of recently used jock straps and sweat socks reached out to claim our sensory orifices. Layered throughout the junior high boys' locker room came additional smells; fumes from still-damp show costumes, escaping, rising from just-unzipped hang-up bags like steam from the grates in a New York City sidewalk; and various sprays like Right Guard under-arm deodorant and Polo. It's a wonder I can even breathe today. I've done hard time in Hairsprayville.

As our eyes meet, we discuss anything out of the ordinary we need to know. We focus ourselves. The stage or gym floor is set. The sound tested. The speaker cords, pedals, and wires taped to the floor with gleaming fresh duct tape. Props are at the ready. Instruments tuned and mics placed in the best possible position to capture the "live" sound of an early morning rock and roll onslaught. Our small-but-mighty platoon of men, a band of brothers, is poised to capture this assembly. We leave our thoughts unspoken: "Attack those little suckers and slay them!" Not even a nervous student body president mispronouncing our name could hold us back.

If we were going to have fun…then they were going to have fun. It was that simple. Sure, we were going

A Free Fare group and crew pose in the boys' locker room, 1977

to posture and prance but not as though we were above them. Our whole countenance would reach out to them. We would not turn our backs on them and jam as though we were in a little club and they were relegated to looking on from afar. Our smiles were a mile wide. Kick it, brother. For the next forty minutes, this is our school. Own it.

We are on! Hit after hit, the songs sweep like a tidal wave over the unsuspecting crowd. Just an hour ago, they were riding the school bus wishing they were back home in bed. And now—music from Loggins and Messina, Edgar Winter, Chicago, The Rolling Stones, Grand Funk, Free…and on it goes. Throw in a little humor…make fun of the principal…and beat a hasty retreat for the sanctuary of that bastion of manliness…the boys' locker room.

I have been naked in some of the best boys' locker rooms in the country. I spent most of the '70s performing assemblies. In how many rooms with that title over the door, BOYS LOCKER ROOM, have I dressed and undressed? Seven years, averaging a couple hundred schools a year, I would guess the real answer would be close to 1,500. The scenario was the same in every one of them.

It didn't matter whether the group changed; the plan stayed the same. Smack 'em in the face. WOW 'em immediately. Sustain the WOW for forty minutes...then disappear. Sometimes three schools or four shows a day.

And afterward...when there are only minutes in the schedule to change back into street gear, gather a little band of volunteers to tear it all down and load up the vehicle, grab the atlas and make our way to the next mind-molding mill, we can look forward to...you guessed it...another boys locker room experience.

» Ralph Watkins (1980–1985):

I didn't make the cut.

[Ralph Watkins was a young man full of youthful confidence. He and his sister, Connie, had grown up with Showcase from the beginning. He felt a certain amount of privilege, as if he had a free pass and could jump in whenever it pleased him. He found out the hard way that he did not have such a pass. Ralph went to the rehearsal camp one summer to audition, as a formality, really. He was sure he was already in. He wasn't.]

I didn't make the cut. I wasn't selected. I grew up around these people! I thought they all knew me; surely, they could find a spot for me. But no, I didn't make it. Lance came to me to deliver the news. He said, "Sorry but we didn't select you." His words of encouragement to me were, "Whatever it's worth, we really were looking for someone that had enough for us to work with." *[Smooth, Lance, very smooth.]*

So, I thought, *those guys are jerks. If they call me back, I'm going to tell them, "Whatever."* About two weeks into the tour in September, they call me.

"This guy is not cutting it. Do you want to go take his place?"

"Absolutely, when do I leave?" So much for "whatever."

So, I went out to join the Fincher Freedom Jam. I had gotten a video of the assembly show and had practiced all the lines. I knew the show cold. I didn't know squat about most of the songs they were singing, but I did have the program down. Lance took me out there to plug me into the show, and introduced me to all of their band members.

Now, when we had to do the first night show, I was scared to death. I didn't know any of the songs and I'm thinking, *How am I going to do this for two hours?* I let Lance know my feelings.

He said, "If you do die onstage tonight, it won't be the last time." That's Lance's encouragement! *[Tell it how it is, Lance.]*

ROAD WARRIORS

*Failure isn't a death sentence.
It's inevitable; a starting point. A classroom.*

Now, our manager, Mayron Fincher, is a tough dude. He broke his neck in a semi-professional football game. If there was any person that worked harder to please the office staff, I don't know who that would be. He was overbearing, very rough. He would just blanket everyone in the group. When he would walk into the room, we would all jump. You would not want to be on his bad side.

After the first assembly, Mark Warfel, the lead singer, came over to me, touched my shirt in the center of my chest, and said, "Hey dude, what's on your shirt?"

I said, "I'm not going to fall for that trick," knowing that he would bring his hand up and hit me on the nose when I looked down at it. It's something we did all the time. But when we lined up to do the "Ten to 7" Bible study, which we did before every night show, ten minutes before 7 p.m., I don't know what demon came into me, I have no idea, but I looked over at Mayron and I said, "Holy cow, didn't you clean your tie?" As I touched his shirt, he looked down at his tie, and I brought my hand up and hit him on the nose.

We were all in shock. We were all frozen. Clocks stopped. Nothing was stirring, not even a mouse. I thought, *My life is going to end right now.* I'm thinking, *Why did I do that? Where did that come from?*

The rest of the guys thought, *Oh boy, we're going to see someone die right now.* There was a pause, which seemed like an hour. It couldn't have been more than a few seconds.

Then Mayron said, "Boy, that was a good one."

WOW! I'm not sure how I survived that. George Floyd was our drummer and was perpetually on Mayron's bad side; he could do no right. He said to me, "I have no idea how you got away with that."

» Steve Soderquist (1983-1985):

Alvin and the Chipmunks

After my first year with YAS, I went home to take a break for the rest of the summer. I got the call that I was invited back the following year and, of course, I returned. I was going to be a Showcase "vet," and for the first time in my life, I felt worthwhile. I was a contributor to something much bigger than I was. I don't remember where we were, the school, the principal, or if it was a first show, second show, or any other little details, but I sure remember the moment when "the rap" part of the day show turned into one of the greatest memories of all.

Here are some specifics: On drums, Dirck Parsons; guitar, Craig Wiggins; bass, John Massey; lead vocals, Joe Theille; me on keyboards; and our manager and sound guy, Jeff Pluth.

Now, it was my job to do the day show rap, which was different from the night show. It was pre-scripted and to be followed to the letter, a word-for-word account on the benefits of staying clean and away from drugs and alcohol. We had specifically arranged that Joe, our singer, would be at my keyboards during my rap, and, at a certain point in the speech, would hit the Play button on my Korg M1 synthesizer. This would begin the opening to the song, "When It's Love" by Van Halen. All Joe had to do was hit that Play button and pretend to be playing the notes. Easy enough. We had done this countless times before and were proud to say, up until this day, without a hitch. I got to deliver the rap, and Joe got to impress the crowd with his prowess on the keys.

However, on this particularly fine afternoon, Joe accidently hit the Tempo Up button. This would not have been such a dire situation if he only hit it once. Dirck was more than capable of getting us back on proper beat when I switched back over; but no…Joe, panicking now, kept trying to fix it, thus hitting it more, and more, and more, until it was cruising along at about Mach-5, or for the sake of reference, about the speed of a hamster's heart.

At first, I just looked over at him as I gave the rap; then as he sped up, I was sped up, trying to keep up with this maniacal pace while Van Halen was being butchered a la Speed Racer over there at the keys. By now, all the kids in the audience looked like they'd had a shot of Novocain, and I'm sure were wondering why I was up there talking about not doing drugs while we all looked like the poster children for addiction out on a day-pass. When I looked over again and saw Joe furiously pretending to play the songs at a blistering pace, I started laughing through my speech. I couldn't even finish. I Alvin the Chipmunk'd a "Thank you and God bless," while Joe walked away from my keyboards with an expression that said, "*Whew! That wasn't easy!*" During all this, Jeff Pluth—our supporter, our mentor, our leader—was almost under the soundboard due to the fact he was laughing so hard. Oh yeah, good times.

» Lance Abair (1972–1983):

Dixie Donuts

I also had the opportunity of exposing a few groups that played Dayton, Ohio, to a place called Dixie Donuts. The owner of the place had a wild African mongoose in the back of the store in a cage. When prompted, he would bring the cage out front to show the mongoose to a whole new group of guys. It was a menacing-looking case, all dark inside. You couldn't get a good look at the mongoose. All you saw was a little bit of fur in the back. He told all of us that the mongoose is the only animal that can kill a cobra snake. He told us that the mongoose had razor sharp teeth that bite at a very high rate of speed. While telling us this he was scratching the bottom of the cage to make a noise, like the mongoose might be moving. During this time, all the guys were getting up closer to the front wire of the cage to try to get a look. At the supreme moment, he pulled a latch on the back, and the top of the cage flew open, flinging a big furry thing right at them. Some of the guys actually seemed able to fly. Everybody freaked. It was always a beautiful moment to expose a new band to Dixie Donuts. Those who were privileged to witness this will never be able to forget it.

I do love a good restaurant prank. The location was a restaurant somewhere in Kentucky. I was traveling with one of the bands and we had stopped for dinner at a generic mom-and-pop restaurant with a large round table that held our entire entourage.

The waitress was in the process of taking orders, and was about five persons away from me. Everyone had a menu in front of him. I turned to the person sitting next to me and gave him the following instructions: "When the waitress gets to the person next to you, I want you to turn to me. In a normal tone of voice, I want you to say, "Look! They have filet mignon here!"

When the waitress reached the necessary position at the table, he exclaimed to me, "Look! They have filet mignon here!"

I turned to him and said, "Naw, I'm not in the mood for fish tonight."

The waitress heard this, came unglued and shouted to us, "THAT'S NOT FISH!" It worked and we all had a good laugh. It's the little things.

» Wes Turner (1972-1973):

Caught in Canandaigua

Creeps. Slime bags. Longhaired hippie freaks. Drug dealers. What in the h&%! are they doing on my road? You could almost read these thoughts in his eyes, as he took off his reflective sunglasses that must have been standard issue to all cops back then.

It was the fall of 1972 and our white bread truck with Florida tags lumbered along State Route 20, which ran parallel to the New York State Thruway and across the tips of the Finger Lakes. The truck looked terribly out of place, like it was avoiding the toll booths for some dark, sinister reason, slinking from shadow to sign to scrub.

Yes, we were longhairs…yes, a couple of us were creepy looking. But, we were dressed in our finest Michael Braun street clothes (as opposed to our outrageous Michael Braun show creations), and our mission on that fine morning was anything but sinister. Our "he-ain't-heavy-he's-my-brother"-hood, our treat-people-like-you-would-like-to-be-treated, total rock and roll love message, was about to be unleashed on the unsuspecting and somewhat mushy minds that made up the youth of the local high school.

Thinking back now, I wonder if things would have been just fine if we had answered his questions with polite, reserved responses instead of insinuating he stopped us just because of hippy drug dealer profiling. Actually, only one of us did the insinuating and answering. That was our major mistake: leaving the talking to the short, fiery, know-it-all, doesn't-respond-well-to-authority-anyway guitar player.

Before we knew it our butts were out and behind the van unloading our equipment on the berm, without any school roadies to help, trying to prove we just wanted to get to the school, which by now was probably wondering where we were. Obviously, the good officer did not find anything out of the ordinary, except some smelly show clothes. I guess he could have gotten us for polluting the air and impersonating rock stars, but I believe he checked with someone from said high school, who convinced him to let us proceed.

The story has a happy ending. We invited him to the night show…and he came! Our conversations with him after the gig were quite different. Just goes to show, "don't judge a book by its cover" goes both ways.

» Wayne Anderson (1970–1976):

KABOOM! BOO! STOP!

I think it was 1973. Steve Thomas was the drummer in my band and Dave Hansen was the funnyman. He could sing, but humor was his thing. Someone booked us in a Christian high school—a very conservative crowd. Now, in our day, we didn't have master volumes on our tube amps. They did not exist in those days. We were loud. We sounded like the Rolling Stones, with no breakers.

Here we are in this wooden building. We had to go upstairs carrying the Hammond B3 up the fire escape, which weighed about four hundred pounds. We were some fun-loving young guys that had no idea what we were about to get into. We're ready to play, in a café-torium of some sort. We were going to shake this place!

We open up and play our first number, then notice, in the back, the teachers were giving us some strange looks, and the band started falling apart behind me. I just kept playing as if everything was fine. Now, Steve Thomas is an excellent drummer, but I heard a *KABOOM!* I turned around and some older guy, a physics teacher, is wrestling with our drummer. He has Steve by his left arm trying to get him to stop, but Steve knows the show must go on no matter what. So, he is hitting the drum with his right hand, trying to keep the rhythm going. All the while Gary Kopco is playing the guitar and trying to negotiate with the principal at the same time. The kids in the audience are yelling "BOO, BOO!" Were they booing us, or the teacher? We didn't know!

The principal finally steps forward with his hand outstretched and says, "STOP. STOP! We're not doing this anymore!" Now, we're still playing, and Gary is still trying to negotiate. The song is finished. Gary is negotiating while the tape starts up playing "Guitarzan," our big comedy number.

This guy was having such a fit, believing that we were a satanic rock band. The principal stepped forward and said, "I've had it. Turn everything off!" At that moment, Dave Anson, who played the part of Tarzan in the skit, does something that he'd never done before. He takes his shirt off, comes running in between us, and starts beating on his chest and screaming like Tarzan.

Now, taking your shirt off at a conservative Christian school was too much. We had to power down. But, the kids threatened to burn the school down if we didn't get to play! The school had so many phone calls they finally negotiated and made up with us, letting us do the night concert.

» Larry Butler (1975-1984):

Breaking Into the Big Time

I have to tell you, my years with Young American Showcase included some of the best times of my life. It actually changed my life and provided me with many lifelong lessons and skills. We spent three tours managing, six years booking, and a couple of years in the home office. I have fond memories of the whole time, but I have to say the three years touring provided the most exciting times and some incredible memories. I could spend hours telling story after story and not begin to cover them all. I would like to tell you about one particular event that was absolutely magical. Before I get into the heart of it, let me tell you a little bit about Dave Hayes and just how special he was, and is.

Dave had, probably still has, a unique gift, and was a people magnet. Typically, we went into a school, and there would be a little lull in the gym before the stage crew was assembled. Barely moments would pass before a group of kids gathered around Dave, hanging on his every word. He would just talk and carry on and the crowd would get larger and larger. Inevitably, I would have to break it up just to get the truck unloaded. When we went to the movies, if the film hadn't started yet, it wouldn't be long before Dave would be in front of the whole theater entertaining everyone. Dave was an incredible impressionist. He could watch you for just a few minutes and peg you exactly. But in these impromptu public performances, Dave was just being himself. He has a unique gift of communication, and people would just enjoy listening to him. So, let me get to this story and lay a little groundwork for it. We had been staying in Oakland, California for a couple of months playing schools around the San Francisco area.

If I remember correctly, it was probably spring break that messed our schedule up; we had to bounce down to Phoenix for a week of shows before we had a few days off ourselves. As anyone who has been on the road with Showcase knows, you work hard. On weekends (if you can call one day off a weekend) and when we had time off, we liked to go somewhere and do something special.

We had planned to jump over to Lake Tahoe after our week in Phoenix. Now, Lance had been drilling us. He insisted that, if we went to Tahoe, we must—absolutely must—see Wayne Newton. Wayne Newton was "Mr. Entertainment," and Lance had us pumped about seeing him and the way he performed. We made the trip to Tahoe and were able to catch Hoover Dam on the way. We got a room at some little cottage-type place, usual for our YAS budget. We all cleaned up and got ready for the show. Here is where it starts getting interesting. It must have been the Lord telling me that Dave was going to get on stage with Wayne Newton that night. I mean, I just knew it was going to happen. We all gathered at the truck and here comes Dave. He had this grey turtleneck sweater thing that he wore all the time. I mean, it was like a uniform. I said, "Dave, you can't wear that; you're getting on stage tonight with Wayne Newton. Go and get your white shirt and your show jacket with all your props so that you'll be ready."

Rack card from the show, courtesy of Paul Turner

Dave, always humble, said, "Naw, man!" Rich Thomas added his insistence that Dave bring his props, and the rest of the band joined in. I said, "Go and change!" He went to put on his show clothes, not because he believed he would perform, but because, in Showcase, you do what your manager tells you to do.

We got to the theater for the midnight show and were beyond excited. I tipped the maître d' and said we wanted a table right down front. He took us to a table that butted right up against the stage. I mean, the guys on the ends could literally rest their elbows on it. I am sure there was some kind of warm-up act or something, but I just don't remember. What I do remember is that Wayne Newton came out and did his opening number, microphones flying all over the stage, communicating like crazy, and we were right there with him. He cut off the song, welcomed everyone, and said, "You all are going to get a great show tonight and let me tell you why. These guys right down here (pointing at us) are pushing me." With that he said, "Who are you all, and where are you from?"

Rich Thomas, without even a thought, said, "We are a band from St. Petersburg, Florida, and this is Dave Hayes, our impressionist."

Wayne smiled. "You do impressions? Come on up and do one for us." I am not making this up. Every word is exactly how it happened. Dave jumped up and ran onto the stage. Wayne asked him about what we did, and after hearing a short explanation about playing schools around the country, Wayne said, "So you do impressions; who would you like to do for us?" Then he handed Dave the microphone.

Dave took the mic and went straight into a perfect Bill Cosby. The crowd went nuts, standing ovation, and all with Dave standing hands outstretched, palms up, toes over the edge of the stage, egging on the response from the crowd like only a true Showcase vet can do. As things quieted a little, Wayne urged him to do another. With that, Dave broke into Howard Cosell and Mohammed Ali, which again ended in thunderous applause. Then Wayne, getting the microphone back, said, "Will you do one more for us?"

Dave responded, "How about Sammy Davis Jr.?"

David Hayes. Photo courtesy of Paul Turner

At this point, Wayne handed the mic back to Dave and asked, "You do Sammy?"

Dave taking the mic said, "Yes, but you have to introduce me" as he handed the mic back to Wayne and walked off stage right, shouting "Candy Man" to the band.

Wayne Newton was blown away by this young kid, just out of high school, taking command of the show. Wayne just stood there dumbfounded with a bewildered look on his face. The band started vamping "Candy Man" and after a dramatic pause (he is quite the pro), Wayne said, "What have I done... will I ever get my show back?" The crowd roared with laughter as the band continued vamping and Wayne rolled into Sammy's intro: "Ladies and Gentlemen, we are happy to have with us tonight, straight from the Sands Hotel, please welcome,

Mr. Sammy...Davis...Jr.!" Now, I must, if you will excuse me, take a sidebar right here. No disrespect to Dave at all; he had an awesome talent, truly a gift, as I have already mentioned. Dave, however, at that time, was not a great singer. He has since become an extremely accomplished singer, but then, not so much. All that to say, we did "Candy Man" in our show every day, and we always did it in the same key—not the key Wayne's orchestra was vamping. (I mean, we are not talking about a five-piece ensemble; we're talking a big band sound with horn section, rhythm, percussion, the whole nine yards!) Well, here comes our "Sammy" out onto the stage in that unmistakable gait and mannerism Sammy was known for. Dave begins: "Who can make the sun rise...sprinkle it with dew..." but singing in his own key! By the downbeat of the word "sprinkle," the whole orchestra changed keys to match Dave, who sailed smoothly through the finish of that routine. I say all that to let you know just how magical the whole night was. Dave completely blew the audience away, another standing ovation. It was incredible.

Wayne did take his show back, and gave us the show we came to see. That was incredible too. At the end of the show, Wayne's assistant came up and said that Wayne wanted to thank us for coming, he wanted to pick up our tab, and said, "Wayne would like to see you backstage." Well, we all took a step forward... but he pointed to Dave and said, "Just him." Dave spent about an hour chatting with Wayne in his dressing room. We were happy to just hang out and bask in the glory of the evening. It was quite a night. There you have it. How Dave Hayes got his break into the Big Time. That evening paved the way and allowed Dave to go back and meet Wayne again after his Showcase days, which led to Wayne helping him get started.

Sammy Davis Jr. attends one of Dave's shows.
Photo courtesy of Paul Turner.

Dave would add that he initially refused Wayne's offer to help, but later Wayne sent a scout out to see a show. Fast-forward to 1991. Dave was performing as Sammy across the country in major theaters and casinos, cruise ships, and eventually headlining as Sammy in "The Rat Pack" show, which traveled the world for several years. Sammy Davis Jr. himself saw Dave's act in Atlantic City and commented, "That was the best singing impersonation of me I've ever heard." Dave is regarded as one of the best tribute artists in the world.

» Dave Kennedy (1980–1981):

Destiny

My story starts with a young man who heard about a fully endorsed touring company that was on the road full time, and I was determined to find out how to join and fulfill my dream of making a living doing what I loved, playing the drums. I had never seen a Showcase band but had heard about it from friends who had. Somehow, I got the phone number and reached out to them. I was not aware it was a "religious" seed-planting organization. I put together an audition tape, fielded questions about my faith, and exaggerated about how much I was involved in church. My dad had been a Church of Christ preacher at one time, but he had passed away unexpectedly in '76. I had gone astray from my faith after that, and was a rebellious teen. Without a father figure, I had some trouble with discipline and was not attending school. I had some run-ins with the law, but, thankfully, was never arrested. I told the Showcase rep what I thought were the right answers, but was not exactly truthful. Needless to say, I did not get the call to join. Later on that year around Christmas, I received a call that one of the drummers was not returning from Christmas break. I would be a last-minute addition to the Loredo Freedom Jam, on tour in Louisiana. It was a dream come true! I had no idea of what was ahead and how much my life would change from the influence and experience that Showcase would provide. I had a lot to learn!

We hit the ground running with up to fifteen shows a week all over Louisiana. We worked hard on our show under the tutelage of Stan Arthur, Lance Abair, and a visit from Lowell Lytle. We were not having much success in Louisiana because our band was not on the funky side and, in a surprise move, the company switched our band with a band touring in Indiana. I will never forget our first show there. The schools were brand new with state-of-the-art auditoriums, and when we ran out on stage to a jumping, standing ovation, we were beyond thrilled! They loved the show and it was so exciting to have all our hard work on the show come to fruition. I had heard of the summer camp that Showcase had every year, and was hoping to be invited back, where I could learn from the book of entertainment concepts taught during that time.

[Indeed, Dave was invited back, and over time, came to grips with his faith. After Showcase, Dave went on to enjoy a notable career in professional music as well. He wrote:]

The concepts I learned and the experience I had in Showcase led me on my path of destiny to travel to more than fifteen different countries and be signed to two major record label deals and entertain millions of people throughout my career. I do not feel I would have had any success without its guidance. Lowell Lytle and his people at Young American Showcase literally changed my life forever and for this, I will always be truly thankful!

I came to believe that a higher power was in control of my life and all I needed was the faith to believe. I learned how to speak and not be intimidated, and truly believe that experience changed me for the better. I have tried to be a good influence with my family and band members and still feel I have a positive, "make it happen" attitude to this day. The mission worked. I am living proof. I was so young, and if not for this company's guidance, I don't think I would have made it.

["The show must go on" was an extension of the "Make it happen" mantra, and very few bands escaped the inevitable test of trying to play through illness, injury, and other difficult circumstances. Following are a few examples that demonstrate the guys' commitment:]

» Bobby (Kingfish) King (1971-1975):

Nosebleed Section

There was a time that I was in a three-piece band with Gary Kopco on bass and Rosco Cooper on guitar. If one guy leaves the stage, you've lost one third of the band. I was a 128-pound "old" guy, the oldest person in Showcase. I was in my mid-twenties—I even had a beard. Now, there's a point in the show where you ask the audience if they would like to hear more music, and you thrust the microphone out to the audience as if you're throwing a football, in order to get a resounding response of "YES!" Well, I knew that part was coming up soon; however, I had a problem from time to time with my nose bleeding. This happened to be one of those times.

Now, on the end of the microphone is a muff made out of foam. Its purpose is to cut down some of the wind, but this day, it had a new purpose.

I can't leave the stage because "the show must go on." My nose starts to bleed, so I leaned forward as I was singing and pressed my nose against the muff, which is now turning red, soaking up all the blood. Kopco has no idea what is happening. Rosco is playing away on his guitar. I'm singing my heart out, and blood is running into the muff. I mean, this was a runner. In my mind, I thought that if I would just concentrate, I could get it to stop. Obviously, that did not work. After about four minutes, this muff was filling up. It was saturated.

Now it gets to the part where you ask the question, "Do you want to hear some more music?" The microphone has a cord hanging from it, and my thumb accidentally hit that little clip that released the cord. The microphone, along with its blood-soaked muff, took off like a missile and hit a little girl wearing a white blouse, who was sitting in the front row. *SPLAT*. You've got the picture. My blood was running down the front of her blouse.

Another time, my nose started bleeding while I was playing bass. I had nowhere to hide and no hands available to staunch the flow. Gary was banging away on the drums. Rosco was going nuts on the guitar. With just the three of us, I could not stop playing bass. *I've got to keep playing,* I thought, *but the audience does not want to see blood running from my nose!* So, I ran behind the curtain, got flat on my back, and kept playing. The principal was standing backstage and saw me on the floor. He must have thought, *What in the world kind of band is this?*

»TJ Klay (1977-1979):

The night show that must go on

The Augello Free Fare was playing a high school in Charleroi, Pennsylvania, 2,300 students, and we were doing the Star Wars skit. It was my job to go out and get the "rough and tough athlete," and he just happened to be sitting in the top row of the bleachers, just as far away as possible. I got up there, but he did not want to come with me, so, the guy sitting next to him grabbed his legs, I grabbed him under the armpits and we proceeded to carry him down the stairs—a very bad idea!

The guy who had him by the legs reached the floor first, and let go. I was still on the fourth step, and fell over the guy we were carrying. When I peeled my face off the gym floor, my foot was on backward. They carried me back on stage and set me on the drum riser. I played the rest of the show with a broken leg, though we didn't realize how bad it was until after the show. This was the second week of our nine-month tour. I spent three days in the hospital, a week in the hotel room, and then I sat on a chair on the edge of the drum riser for six weeks, then on a stool back on the front line. I was on crutches until I came back after our Christmas break.

Fast-forward to the last three weeks of tour, with a new manager, Larry Smith. I was walking up the motel stairs to leave for our night show, when my ankle gave out. I fell on the stairs and broke two bones in the same foot of the leg I had broken at the top of our tour. We played our evening show, had two shows back to back at the same school the next day, did one afternoon show, then the manager took me to the hospital while the rest of the band set up for our "night show that must go on" that night.

I came back with another cast.

Now, the next day, Larry had to call the office to tell them about what happened to me. This is exactly the conversation, and totally true:

Lowell answers the phone and says, "Hey Larry, what's going on? Did TJ break his leg again?"

Larry: [gulp] "Yeah..."

You can't make this stuff up.

[Not all of the difficult circumstances involved physical pain. When you throw four or five young, headstrong strangers together into a never-ending and extremely difficult circumstance, you are going to have some personality conflicts. It was the manager's job to help the guys learn to work together and forge positive relationships as quickly as possible, but sometimes that was a nearly impossible task. At one point, as we have mentioned, all of the bands studied Tim LaHaye's Spirit-Controlled Temperaments *together on the road, one of the tools the spiritual director of the organization used to get everyone on the same page. Different bands used other methods, and all bands met together daily to talk, pray, work through their issues, and prepare themselves for the challenge ahead. TJ goes on to describe one such "temperament clash":]*

In my first band, my bandmate Stan Arthur and I did not "get on" well, and it was public knowledge. I "diagnosed" him as being "too choleric" (I learned that term from reading Tim LaHaye's *Spirit Controlled Temperaments*) and, to quote Johnny Ringo, "Poor soul, he was just a little too high-strung." In turn, he was frustrated by my Midwestern demeanor and laid back nature—a poor match, to say the least, that affected the entire band all year long.

Now, after our first year, I was sure I would be invited back. I spent the summer break learning all the songs on the pre-camp tape and practicing my rock and roll moves in front of a big mirror in our basement. I worked hard, every day, six to eight hours a day, and I WAS READY!

About a week before camp, I got the call saying that there wasn't a position for me. Needless to say, I was crushed and embarrassed. My family was supposed to drop me off at rehearsal camp, and then go on their summer vacation. What would I say to them?

Little did I know that Stanley got the same call.

About two weeks into camp, Lowell called me and said they were in a jam. If I still wanted to come, there was a place for me, but there was one catch: I would have to work with Stanley again. I listened to Lowell try to explain a few things, and just interrupted him and said, "Okay!"

Stanley got that same call too, but there was one catch: he would have to work with *me* again... and he also said, "Okay!"

[This two-week delay was a sobering reality check for both headstrong young men. As talented as they were, no managers wanted to take them on together. Did God

orchestrate their conditional reunion, or did Lowell and the leadership team? Either way, something had to change, or they would be sent home. This time, they knew what was at stake.]

That second tour with Augello Free Fare, God did something amazing with Stanley and me. We forged a friendship that remains strong to this day, and every so many years we get to hook up for some good food and drink.

Fast-forward to the big Showcase Reunion in Florida in 2007. A stage was set up with full band equipment, and former Showcasers got the chance to play again with their former bandmates. I got to be on stage with all but one of my first-year band mates. Stanley and I sang "Dust in the Wind," complete with the synth strings and a harmonica solo. When the second verse came around, I walked over and put my arm around his shoulder. I praise the Lord for that restored relationship. Very few people there knew just exactly how far we had come.

All bands experienced some kind of challenge such as fractures and other injuries, illnesses, and robberies, encounters with the law, equipment failures, dangerous situations, and temptations of all kinds. Before Showcase, their first response may well have been, "I can't continue. I need a break. I don't have it in me." Sometimes life circumstances changed and they needed to be home. A few band members did opt to go home mid-year, were sent home, or, physically, emotionally, or spiritually just could not continue. For the most part, however, when trials would come up, these young men and women learned, to a person, that they were capable of far more than they ever realized.

» Glenn Quiggins (1982-1983):

Jenga

We were doing a night show at Gladstone, Michigan, in the Upper Peninsula, playing in a theater, with all the rows of curtains you can raise and lower. I had a crazy high drum riser, three levels high, maybe eight feet square. "Freebird," the last song of the show, was over; I turned to step off the back of the riser onto a makeshift staircase of road cases. I took one step and the whole Jenga staircase fell, and me with it. I ended up knocked unconscious, hidden between two rows of curtains.

Everybody was out front signing posters when someone asked where I was. Around this same time, the guy that was teching for me found me behind the drums. The EMTs were called; I was strapped to a board and fitted with a neck brace, and rolled out on a gurney. Seeing the scared and confused faces of the audience, Chris Gellini noted, "The high school girls shed many a tear, thinking the worst." I spent some time in the hospital, but other than a few bruises, I was okay.

[One important job upon arrival at a school was locating three 20-amp grounded power sources. This next story illustrates why:]

»Jeff Siebert (1989-1991):

Rubber Boots

One time we were at a school in Red Ball, Georgia (or at least that was the name of the school), when a "shocking" thing happened to our lead guitar player, Chris Turnbull. We could not find one grounded outlet in the gymnasium. We figured out a way to get power and get everything going. Chris played the role of the patriot in the show, and did all the narrating. He stepped up to the microphone and started to sing. Apparently, his lips touched the microphone, and suddenly I couldn't hear him singing any more. I looked to my left and he was gone! Chris was about five feet back from the microphone, flat on his back, holding his guitar and shaking as if he was having a seizure. He had just been electrocuted and was out like a light! His guitar strings were burnt! We carried him backstage and, while our manager, Monte Godfrey, ran back to take care of Chris, we ran back out to continue the show. We went into a drum solo. I went in to a keyboard solo. Ten minutes later, there was still no Chris, and the kids were just looking at us, so I said, "Let's divide this room in half. Everybody on the right side say "Freedom" and everyone on the left say "Jam!" "Freedom—Jam! Freedom—Jam!" Back and forth we went. Finally, Monte came over to me and said, "Stall a little longer." No one knew at the time but, when Chris got electrocuted, he lost all of his body functions in his pants! To this day, we think he survived only because he was wearing rubber boots as part of his costume.

»Gary Kirk (1985-1986):

Duct tape and never giving up

I have many stories of the diesel fuel gelling in Wisconsin, blowouts in Michigan, getting stuck in Mississippi, breakdowns in Tennessee, and plain ol' running out of fuel. There are stories such as the time I put an adjustable wrench through a monitor speaker while making repairs, planning out a trip that only gave us five minutes to set up before showtime, and the assistant manager filling the diesel truck with regular gasoline. I have stories of Lowell pulling me aside and almost sending me home, my manager being so disappointed in me that I vowed to never let that happen again, then telling me that he hated to critique me because he was my friend. I saw St. Louis, Chicago, Milwaukee, Detroit,

Atlanta, and New York City. I drove through the night, like a zombie, getting us lost. We watched the sun set as an orange orb, mesmerized, while traveling in our Iveco through Illinois. We watched huge, frozen chunks of ice in Lake Michigan. We cooked out at a hotel by the shore of Lake Superior. We went to the top of the Sears Tower and the World Trade Center. The best pizza of my life? Chicago. My first exposure to Greek food was in Detroit. I got free cymbals when mine cracked and u-joints for my DW pedal with a note from a Showcase staffer telling me "Do not attempt to smoke!" My drum cases were duct tape-reinforced cardboard boxes. The Simmons drum module made me bleed, and once seemed to have a life of its own after a Nerf football bounced off my face and hit it.

I felt like I was probably the only introvert to get into YAS in its entire history. I remember at the end-of-year camp so many other musicians marveling at me as if I were some sort of Showcase anomaly and I felt like I was. I struggled, fought, and never gave up. I made lifelong friendships and found a mentor that not only helped me become a better musician but also helped me become a better person. Brian completed what my father and older brother left incomplete. If I could talk to him again, I would simply say … thanks. I met students that were as touched as I was when Free Fare came to my high school. The best part, though, was the change that came about in me from this "Christian Rock and Roll Military Academy." Without a doubt, this was one of the happiest times of my life. It was full of exponential growth and experience that made me better. I'd like to thank Lowell for all of it.

» Wes Turner (1972-1973): The Showcase Way

Acolytes training in the Florida dark
Crave approval from the pope of Pinellas Park.
Wide-eyed sleep-deprived training camp fools
New axe, new amp, new truck, new tools.
Abair's on…like white on rice,
Angst-led fear dread-sweat damp price
Of doing it
The Showcase way.

Wizards from Oz,
Personal life on pause,
Kick-starting little girls' dreams
On a daily basis.
Shock 'n awe-some stage sight,
Rock 'em, slam 'em, bring 'em back at night.
Fast-food junkies,

Amp-jumpin' monkeys,
Taking names and kickin' in doors,
The Showcase way.

Every night a different town.
Breadtruck bums from the edge
(pun intended).
Hobbits with hair…munchkins on spray,
Are you sure Led Zep started this way?
Superbad color fad life in Extreme
Livin' that school boy rock star dream
Another day, another town…
Time to go share His love,
In a Supercharged show,
The Showcase way.

Lowell, thanks for your expertise and willingness to provide an avenue for "the lost boys" to tell their stories. I think, to a person, we would all call the years on the road, whether successful or trying, magical and life-changing, both for us and for those to whom we performed and witnessed.

PART SEVEN

THE QUESTIONS

Leslie: How're you doing, Lowell?
Lowell: Rippty Dippty.

Showcase members were asked a series of specific questions about their experience:

1. *How did your Showcase experience impact your faith?*
2. *How did your Showcase experience impact your future career and ministry?*
3. *How did your Showcase experience impact your family life and personal growth?*

HOW DID YOUR SHOWCASE EXPERIENCE IMPACT YOUR FAITH?

» Ralph Watkins (1980-1985):

There was a particular time when we were playing in Louisiana that I got sick with something. I was always very thin; I still am. I'm six foot three inches tall right now, and I was the same height when I was in junior high school. When I graduated from high school, I weighed 155 pounds. When I started tour I was 195, but I was losing weight, as if I couldn't eat. We were doing shows, and I was down to 144. I looked like a skeleton starvation experiment, like I was in a concentration camp or something. It was not a healthy thing. So, one day I prayed and said, "Lord, I know you can do anything, so, this is what I'm going to do. I'm going to fast for ten days, and at the end of that I'm going to ask you to put ten pounds on me." I don't know why I even thought this was scriptural.

Days go by and I'm crazy out of my mind with hunger. So, we go and do the night show, and I'm the one that does the rap. After the program, I meet this kid and he starts asking questions about our faith. That might have been the very best testimony-sharing and evangelistic conversation that I have ever had.

We took him into the dressing room and the guys were all chipping in with testimony. When we left the school that night, I was overcome with emotion, as I am right now just thinking about it. God was saying, *I can use you just exactly the way you are, the weight you are, where you are—just get out of my way.* I definitely felt like the Lord was speaking through me when I was talking to this kid and, all of a sudden, this drive to gain weight was gone. It was just lifted and gone from me. It was like, wherever I am, whatever weight I am, it's cool. From there I went to Taco Bell and I think I ate everything I could get my hands on.

» Lance Abair (1972-1983):

As a new Christian, I found it very stimulating to, all of a sudden, be surrounded by people of faith. This was quite new to me. This fellowship continually grew and strengthened my faith.

» Stan Arthur (1977-1990):
Showcase gave me a spiritual foundation that has been the core of my faith since that time.

» Roger Blackington (1970-1971):
Seeing a refreshing way to witness in a world that needs something to identify with opened up the world of evangelism for me.

» Lang Bliss (1978-1984):
I was saved in Showcase. My experience in YAS informed everything I believed for my first and foundational years as a believer.

» Chris Bouvier (1983-1985):
I was not even close to the Lord, until I met the Lytle family. Lowell specifically helped me find the Lord, and I became friends with Jesus Christ.

» Joe Brown (1969-1972):
For me, life on the road that first year with Free Fare was tied to the calendar and the clock. The schedule rarely let up. We typically played three shows a day, one in the morning, another at a different school that afternoon, and the long show somewhere else that evening. We would set up and tear down three times a day, sometimes four. That kind of schedule messes with your sense of time and place. If it's Tuesday, we must be in Bradenton. Oh, this is Wauchula? Then it's Wednesday. So, spiritual life was catch as catch can. Quiet time? What is that?

The spiritual journey for me was wrapped up in the overall experience and the people I was around. It was a long-term transformation, one you don't realize day to day. It's the culmination of all these experiences, the shows, the students who responded, the teaching from Gary Horton and others throughout the Showcase years, the influence of Lowell's seemingly limitless faith, the ups, the downs… all of it melded into life lessons that stick with me—frequently in my subconscious, but they are always there. They have become a part of who I am. And though I've come to believe that God is so vastly larger that I can ever imagine, and the older I get, dogma means less and less while caring for people means more and more… these experiences will always be there, shaping all of life itself.

» John Gunden (1977-):
Perhaps the most influential thing that happened was Mike and Pam Augello's commitment to "Ten to 7"s and John MacArthur Bible teaching. Christ was being formed in me even through all the screaming mee-mees playing with my head. Since then I went on to work with YFC as a youth worker and in

1991, I founded R U Red E? Ministries, dedicated to taking the gospel to a teenage world. Since then, we have seen over 30,000 professions of faith to the glory and praise of God. In 1999, we began a church called the River's Edge, a reformed fellowship, where I serve as pastor, discipling a flock of 200 in the small lakeside town of Caseville, Michigan, population 707! It is wonderful to consider the mosaic of what God does in obedient people like Lowell and Lance and especially Barb Lytle. To think of the souls many of these men would reach in other spheres of influence.

It was Barb who saved me from being gonged in the audition room. My performance was so pitiful Lowell was openly laughing at me, and the others were trying not to! Somehow, she believed in me, and then Lowell believed in me, and then Lance, who was a serious musician! I loved it when he came out to jam with us on the old sax!

Honestly, the generosity of YAS is something to consider, because so many lives have been touched by the gospel of Jesus Christ through all the young Americans they mentored. They were very patient with us. With me. Who does that these days? Because, no one got rich doing it, that's for sure.

Anyway, I am just blessed to have been a part of this fine organization, Young American Showcase; what an honor to serve in such a great effort to reach so many teens. God bless all in the fellowship of the three-ring-circus called Young American Showcase! It was the most exciting, life-altering time of my life!

» Phil Hardley (1974-1987):

[Phil Hardley served many years as a manager, and then as spiritual director.]
The one thing that stands out is "trust"—not trusting family or friends—I am talking about God. I left a good paying job with a McDonald's franchise to come to YAS, which required trust. The message of the first meeting I had with the eight managers was, "We don't have any money to pay you." Everyone had to trust. The last meeting we had as staff thirteen years later was, "we don't have any money to pay you." More trust. During those thirteen years, I was fired three times and quit three times. I think I hold the record. Thank goodness, Lowell and I have long-time family ties and we are still to this day long-time friends. So, my time with YAS was over, but the opportunity to trust God was not. What does a guy with a family of four do without a paycheck? Put on your boots and pray a lot. I started my own business and continued with that fifteen years, until God closed that door. He opened another for eighteen years. All that to say this: God is a whole lot smarter than I am and loves me a lot more than I love Him. Faith and trust in Him is the thing I hold dearest to my heart. Life may kick me in the ass but God has always been there to make sure I have a soft landing. Thanks Lowell and Barb for all the great memories and the friends we made during those years, and for setting us off on a "trust" journey with God.

I remember the day at rehearsal camp the staff all went out to lunch together. Sitting about fifteen feet from us was another Christian group whose leader was going around the nation talking about how bad rock music was and killing the faith and morals of America's teens. Here we were, both groups on the same team but on opposite sides. It struck me that day how different we were, and yet still the same. Lowell wanted to go over and have a "talk" with them but we tied his hands and feet to his chair and kept stuffing biscuits in his mouth. He went away full. Fun day we had, good memories. Seeing the lives that were changed over the years because of YAS, I'm glad I was sitting at our table. A few years before that, I was sitting at the other table. I saw a picture once of the Eagles and Saints praying together after a game; it's kind of like that.

» Wayne Hackett (1969-1972):
At seventeen, I began evangelizing on top of an ice cream parlor roof and I saw lives changed. I never lost that desire to lead people to Christ. All through my secular career, I also produced evangelistic outreaches that are now streamed and televised all over the world.

» Alec Johannson:
Strengthened me greatly and I became a man.

» TJ Klay (1977-1979):
One of the ways Showcase affected my faith was in our "morning glories." Besides going through different study books, we also did things like Tim LaHaye's *Spirit-Controlled Temperament* and the Navigator's "New Topical Memory System." I remember Pam Augello, our manager's wife, and I going through different psalms, rotating every other word back-and-forth... it was a lot of fun but it also really helps you get God's Word down in your heart where it needs to be.

» Alex Lagos (1983-1984):
I was raised Catholic, and accepted Christ while in Showcase. On tour, I would tell others about my experience, and most of them understood.

» Ron Lentini (1970-1985):
It strengthened my faith as I saw God working in lives. It helped me become bolder in sharing my faith.

» Chris Lundquist (1983-1985):
Mostly by the example of Lowell, I learned that faith in God is the foremost important thing in your life. Also, working with other Christians in real-life situations put "wheels" to my faith.

» Don Morrissette (1972-1975):
The greatest gift I received during my first tour with Free Fare was my salvation.

» Steve Soderquist (1983-1985):
It changed it forever. When I found I could be accepted as I was, even the mess I was, it opened my eyes.

» Steve Tharp (1987-1991):
My Showcase experience impacted my faith in so many ways. I learned to rely on the Holy Spirit. I learned to share my faith quickly. I also learned to rely and rest on my relationship with Jesus. And, I learned that I really don't have to eat, sleep, or use the restroom when I'm working for the Lord. I have gone for entire days without having the time to use the restroom. And, I have gone for several days in Showcase without time to eat or sleep, while doing shows and driving the truck in-between.

[Not everyone who worked for Showcase thrived spiritually during their time with Showcase. Some didn't make it and were sent home. Some admittedly managed to "fake it through." Some struggled the entire time with their faith, but the experience stuck with them and impacted them in the years that followed, like our brutally honest friend, Hiroshi.]

» Hiroshi Upshur (1970-1975):
Well, the truth comes out. Before Showcase, I had accepted Christ in my bedroom, watching a Billy Graham event on TV. He warned of hell, dying, and not getting the opportunity to come forward. I didn't want to go to hell. Would a loving God send billions to hell to be tortured for eternity when "God is love"? I didn't know it at the time, but years later, I realized that my decision was based on fear, not love. These things began to haunt me and didn't make sense, but I kept quiet. I was so busy in Showcase concentrating on the show and living with fellow musicians that God and faith took a backseat. Yes, we prayed before shows, but for me it was out of fear. We were kids ourselves, and in that era, kids in the audience with long hair or huge afros and "impress me" attitudes were scary. And being so sleepy from not enough sleep, then giving an assembly speech at 8 in the morning, wasn't the greatest idea. I am a musician. I don't get started until after lunch. Before that, I am as confused as a termite on a yo-yo. But we were kids, so we didn't know better.

I think it was Socrates who said, "The unexamined life is not worth living." I dropped out of college after my first year because of the opportunity to travel in a rock group with Showcase. My point with the quote is that I just didn't have the time to make an effort to examine my beliefs and to grow in that aspect during Showcase. God was someone to run to when you wanted something or someone—a cosmic bellhop. If I got sick, I prayed, "God make me well." Scared? "God help me not to fear." If I didn't get along with a band member or manager, "God help me with that person." "God help us to have a great show." Later on, during some self-inquiry, I realized my relationship with God was one-sided, but during Showcase years, it was all about me. Screaming girls and kids wanting my autograph didn't help. It just grew my ego. Later on, when I got out of Showcase, made it to Hollywood, and was among other great musicians, I realized I had a long way to go. There is plenty of great talent around, which keeps one humble. Showcase was difficult. I believed the hype at the time. We were being developed in many areas, not just musically, but as performers and comedians. Plus, we were getting experiences that one day we would treasure. I did take the time and effort after Showcase to examine my beliefs and take it deeper. I took courses to study great theologians. I studied apologetics and Christian philosophy in LA. So, I had many questions and investigated Christianity at a deep level. I was a seeker of truth, wanting to know if what I believed was true or not. I tested myself by going to Santa Monica Promenade with a fellow apologist named Sammy, who was a Jewish Christian, to get into debates with people there. This was a tough place to engage, but I learned a lot about myself.

HOW DID YOUR SHOWCASE EXPERIENCE IMPACT YOUR FUTURE CAREER OR MINISTRY?

Many Showcase vets weighed in with some overall thoughts about their personal journey through or after Showcase. Joe Brown would agree with Hiroshi that his training, both professional and spiritual, was not complete when he "graduated" from Showcase:

» Joe Brown (1969-1972):

My own life journey has been profoundly affected by two years touring with Young American Showcase. But, my journey has been exactly that—a journey. Today, I am not where I started, nor am I where I was twenty-five years ago. Nor have I arrived at a final destination. Not yet. We are all still on that journey, as long as we breathe.

Who was not affected by the YAS culture of "make it happen"? Some unexpected event occurs on the road. A steel bar your truck ran over is thrown up under the truck and punctures the gas tank, causing gasoline to pour out on the highway as you drive. You pull over and you're stuck in the middle of Nowhere, Maine, miles from Presque Isle—not far from the Canadian border—where you are to play the school the next morning... and it's late at night (all true from a third year Free Fare). You find a pay phone and call Lowell saying you can't make the show tomorrow. He replies, "Call someone. Wake them up. Get a U-Haul truck and transfer the equipment. Get there. Play the show. Make it happen."

Sigh. Okay boys, let's do it.

I mean, what YAS veteran did not recall a similar scene later in life and realize, whatever the obstacle, it *can* be overcome. I just have to do what's necessary to make it happen. I doubt any of us forgot that essential lesson. By the way, we did play that show the next day, albeit short on sleep.

Those of us who continued performing will never forget what we learned, whether it was in church or another cover band playing weddings or community club dances. Never again will I allow too much pause between songs. If I do, Lowell Lytle's voice will boom inside my head, "DEAD AIR!"

My own career consisted of disc jockeying where there really could not be dead air, then working at recording studios, finally managing my own, where keeping things moving and clients happy was of supreme importance. The practical lessons I learned from Lowell Lytle and other great pros with YAS will never leave, as I am sure they have not left others who performed with YAS bands. It is not an overstatement to say those YAS experiences had a huge—if sometimes sub-conscious—impact on my life and work.

» Dave Walker (1983-1991):

With my Showcase journey, I personally witnessed countless lives changed. This strengthened my faith and growth in the Word. I was fortunate to have an amazing manager and wife team. They held us accountable to learn the Word, and our pre-show Bible studies were consistent. Meeting Lowell and the staff, even just learning the history of the company, instilled a feeling inside me, and a commitment similar to being in a military regiment—God's Army!

» Lance Abair (1972-1983):

Showcase was a strong addition to the life I was living. Following Showcase, I went on to become a regional product specialist for Korg, USA, a midi products manager and artist relations for Nord lead synthesizers and Ddrums. Showcase prepared me for doing training at both Korg and Bose, Inc.

» Stan Arthur (1977-1990):

Lowell Lytle's mentorship transformed me from an arrogant child into a Spirit-led young man.

» Gary Horton (1968-71/1978-91):

[You may remember that Gary was in the very first band, which started out with just Gary and Lowell.] Serving in the band was one of the greatest privileges of my life. I was so honored to do what little I was able to do because I didn't have the expertise to do what some of the people that followed could do. I finally stepped down from the group in the early '70s to travel to California to visit my brother, who had just come back from Vietnam. I knew it was time for me to move on. I decided to spend some years serving my country in the United States Army.

From 1972 to 1977, I served in the Army airborne Rangers. I was thirty-one years old when I joined, and later was asked to return to YAS to challenge further the young men that Lowell Lytle and the team had put together each year, a much more professional organization than what we had to start with. I was allowed to come and encourage these young men concerning their priorities in life and relationship to God through Christ. That was also a tremendous highlight in my life.

Since leaving the United States Army, I began speaking in schools as a patriot and as a veteran, and have done so for the past forty-plus years. The adventures God has given me are beyond words! It is because of God's grace, and the people across this country that work with me and allowed me access to the schools across America, that I've been to over seven thousand schools in forty-six states, and I'm still going. I'm still available.

[You can find many inspiring videos of Gary speaking online under "Ranger Gary Horton" and the American Freedom Assembly at youthontrack.org.]

» Roger Blackington (1970-1971):
I've worked in church production, both traditional and contemporary, helping to open up doors to reach people for Christ. I'm an audio specialist now, running sound, and installing for churches throughout Rochester. God has given me a unique ministry of even running sound in bars, showing my Christian faith to the people there. I ran over one hundred shows last year, to the glory of God!

» Lang Bliss (1978-1984):
Because of Showcase, I believed that I was supposed to do music as a calling and career and it gave me an undying tenacity to go for that. I was able to walk through doors because of that experience that I don't think I would have had the faith and experience to walk through. I am still reaping the benefits of all that Showcase did for me.

» Chris Bouvier (1983-1985):
Showcase led me down a better path where I began helping others be successful, and guiding them toward the Lord.

» Ron Lentini (1970-1985):
We ALL learned how to "make it happen!"

» Wayne Hackett (1969-1972):
Eventually I wanted to get off the road and went back to LALA land. The skills I learned in YAS served me well. I went on to a career creating, producing, directing, and acting in television and film in Los Angeles. Those words "You can make it happen" from Lowell built the confidence I needed to get my own

show on network TV, and to continue working my entire life in the sometimes-volatile entertainment business.

» Monty Godfrey (1985-1988):

I recently left a very successful twenty-nine-year career in timeshare marketing. I was either a VP or director for many of those years with Fortune 500 companies such as Wyndham and Hilton. What served me well during my tenure was God-given people skills that many people simply do not possess. While that always came naturally for me as far as I can remember, those skills developed rapidly as I learned and lived the "concepts" that were ingrained in us—the art of non-verbal communication, such as a smile, a gesture, eye contact, etc.

As most people know that study such things, non-verbal communication can get across what you are intimating even more than the words you say. The ability to be comfortable in any setting and make the person I may have been negotiating with feel equally comfortable was key to a lot of my success. After hundreds of shows in front of thousands of people with Showcase, I became fearless in front of people whom I had never met. I gained confidence as well. In business, I was equally at ease, whether I was dealing with a flea market peddler or sitting across the table from someone that was worth $100 million.

From high school to my career, the four and a half years in Showcase taught me so much about life, responsibility, interpersonal relationships, and management, for which I am forever thankful.

» Alec Johannson:

I learned to understand people and learned it took all kinds of people, from all walks of life, to make the world go 'round. No matter how different we look, we all have one thing in common, and that is GOD and JESUS.

» TJ Klay (1977-1979):

Without a doubt, Showcase set the bar for every other musical situation I have ever been in. When you do between two and four assembly shows a day and a ninety-minute concert six nights a week, when you have to leave the hotel in the wee hours of the morning to get to your first show, when there's not always time to stop and eat and you're fined a dollar for every minute you're late (which comes out of your little per diem), you learn a lot of discipline, work ethic, and you learn what an incredible opportunity and dream you are living out. In the very same day, you have the chance to do it again, maybe two or three times, and do it better, learn from your mistakes, hone your craft professionally, and, more importantly, spiritually. You learn to "make it happen."

Just about everything I know about entertaining a crowd, I can trace back to Showcase. The big one for me has always been dividing your audience in sections, three across the front, three across the middle, and three across the back, and you play to those sections. You work each of those sections, and fifty people will feel like you just looked right at them! It's all about making eye contact (even though you can't see past the third row!), and showing your appreciation for them. Go out and love your audience; they'll love you back, but you gotta keep it real, and not take yourself too seriously.

[As others have mentioned, the skills learned on the road with Showcase translated well to almost any other line of work, ministry, or life experience. Gary Kolosey describes how his "graduation" after four and a half years in "Showcase University" prepared him for his future career:]

» Gary Kolosey (1975–1980):

I came to Florida in December of 1975 from Massachusetts to join the second Freedom Jam group, which did a half-year tour. I toured the next two years, then Connie and I got married in the summer of 1978 and put all the wedding gifts in storage to go on the road as group managers for two years. All that came to a screeching halt when the tour ended in summer 1980. By the time I left Showcase in 1980 after four and a half years on the road, I decided to find a traditional job.

I tried a bunch of different jobs, including some failed attempts at getting a business started and a few other projects that didn't seem to work so well. I was also trying to finish school and get my degree. During all of that, Jacob, son number one, came along, so now I had a family to feed. I was desperate. I had to make some money, so was looking to take any job I could.

There were a few weird jobs that were obviously not a good fit, but I needed the money, so I did whatever I had to do. One of the things on my list to try was substitute teaching. I had always thought that teaching was the last thing I wanted to do. I remembered how I treated teachers and did not in any way want to be on the receiving end of that. To my amazement, that substitute job was great! It didn't pay much, but I was so excited about connecting with those kids. I should have figured out that being in front of high school and junior high kids for all those years with Showcase prepared me in ways I could not have predicted.

Each class period was an opportunity to exercise all the Showcase entertainment principles to a small audience of high school students but do it without the band and the clothes. It took a while to translate the stage concepts into the classroom, but I definitely had a set of tools I had been using on stage that became useful, even essential, to teaching success. Things like communication, crowd control, direction and misdirection, love and energy, audience participation, humor, music, and all the ideas we practiced during every show, were there in my toolbox waiting to be used in the classroom.

Just like any tour, however, some classes go well, and others don't. You learn to work with what you have and make the most out of any situation. In general, "make it happen."

I can say now, having retired after thirty-two years in the classroom, that Showcase prepared me for the rigors and challenges of public school teaching in ways I could never have imagined while I was on the road.

More responses to the question about how Showcase impacted participants' future career or ministry:

» Alex Lagos (1983-1984):
Thanks to Showcase, I started a long climb that, along with family, I still see the fruits of today. I never stopped doing what I loved, instead did musical-related activities along with a professional curriculum. Today I focus on music and building guitars. I improved the guitar in many ways; I was the first in LA to build a seven-string that created a trend. I became a master luthier for artists only at Fernández Ibáñez - University of Amsterdam so, it's all good— and still going.

» Chris Lundquist (1983-1985):
Music was what I loved to do, and seeing a Showcase band in high school showed me that I could serve God through music, which I have continued to do.

» Steve Soderquist (1983-1985):
My fiancé and I, Laura Ranger, started our own publication company and called it Foundations, as it is founded on Christ. We accept all genres as, like YAS, we believe we must reach and accept everyone if we're to be effective in spreading the gospel. We are often seed-planters, and always readily available to open our hearts and mouths, as He sees fit.

» Steve Tharp (1987-1991):
Dave Lytle never stopped challenging my faith. I am grateful. When I left Showcase, I joined a band of young teenagers and used my experience to help the band grow from a garage band into the most wanted rock band in the Tri-State, all while sharing the gospel with the band and our fans continually. I have never stopped playing music, working with youth, sharing my faith, and most of all loving Jesus. I've worked at the Songwriters Guild of America and currently work at SESAC helping writers and publishers. Also, I am a worship pastor

who doubles as the youth pastor today at Bell Road Church of the Nazarene in Nashville, Tennessee.

On the fifth Sunday of March 2019, my pastor was asked to speak at a gathering of several black churches downtown in Nashville. Being his worship pastor, it was expected that I would lead worship. When we walked into the church and the pastors on the platform noticed that I was not black, one leaned in close to my pastor and said, "I'll go ahead and lead worship today."

My pastor said, "No. We got this." I walked up to the platform and started leading worship. At first, they were not really open to being led by a white guy with a mandolin. However, I loved them with my eyes, like I learned in Showcase. In other words, I looked everyone in the eyes and smiled at them with the freedom of knowing the truth in Christ. And, one by one, they started worshiping until the entire congregation was worshiping as one. After the service, one of the pastors asked when I could lead again. I thank God for my experience in Showcase, and I use these experiences continually in my life.

» Paul Turner (1976-1978):

During my first "real" career interview post-Showcase, my prospective boss said, "Take this jeweler's pad; if you can perform, let this be your stage." Eight years later, I had his job after he retired as a training supervisor. I supported my family with an eighteen-year career in jewelry management, applying Showcase principles. Now I give music lessons full-time and perform, using those same skills every day. I have continued to apply the principle that music reaches people on a very deep level in my songwriting and ministries over the years. I teach students to choose carefully what they put in their minds, and produce projects designed to reach secular audiences with the gospel by "earning the right to be heard" first, meeting their needs and opening doors through music.

» Hiroshi Upshur (1970-1975):

Just being honest, Showcase had an incredible impact on my future career as a musician. After Showcase, I packed my van and drove from New Jersey to LA to "make it." Within a few months, I got a gig, and hustled my songs, which opened doors to audition with Gary Wright ("Dream Weaver"). I toured with him for seven months, and also got married. Doors opened for me as a studio musician and I learned from working with artists such as the late Michael Jackson, Marvin Gaye, Aretha Franklin, David Foster, Quincy Jones, and more, presently with Paul Anka. Showcase principles played a part in all of that, giving me confidence, and turning me into a good actor. If I could stand in front of a racially divided audience in the South and not be intimidated, I could overcome anything. If I could stand up to a seven-foot Lowell Lytle in a hotel room and say I am not going to do any shows unless the bookings are changed, I could face anyone. Many things happened in the years after Showcase. My life got complicated with marriages and kids and of course, the career as a pro musician, but as mentioned earlier, I did take the time and effort to examine my beliefs and take it deeper.

» Dave Walker (1983-1991):

All my years in Showcase—and there were seven in various positions—helped me achieve many professional highlights in the years that followed. Every aspect of business always returns to what I learned in YAS. Years after Showcase, I had the opportunity to bring Mark Lach, longtime Showcase performer and staff member, and Lowell Lytle himself, into working for RMS *Titanic*, another pathway that God had opened. Through this, Lowell has been able to continue using his voice telling thousands the story of Reverend John Harper, who perished on *Titanic*, but continued preaching salvation until his last breath! I am in awe that Lowell keeps pressing toward the finish line, when God will say, well done my good and faithful servant.

HOW DID YOUR SHOWCASE EXPERIENCE IMPACT YOUR PERSONAL GROWTH AND FAMILY LIFE?

» Lance Abair (1972-1983):
I've been married to my dream girl for fifty-two years. I have gone through some fairly bad health problems, and my faith assisted me in maintaining a positive attitude throughout. It means a lot to know that this world is only a brief stopping point in life. There is a lot left to enjoy knowing that Christ is with me throughout.

» Stan Arthur (1977-1990):
I learned a lot about commitment. I have been married for nearly thirty-nine years.

» Roger Blackington (1970-1971):
YAS allowed me to look at all Christian ministry as a growing adventure rather than "we've always done it that way." I have over thirty years of church ministry behind me now and am still going. My family grew up singing as a group for years, giving my kids the confidence to grow, in both music and their commitment to Christ.

» Lang Bliss (1978-1984):
I went through the scripture memorization course while on the road as well as the Colossians 2:7 course. I began to understand the Word, and what I did learn planted the truth in me. I knew that I had to marry a woman that had the same values and belief in Scripture, and a personal relationship with Jesus.

» Chris Bouvier (1983-1985):
I would not have the wonderful wife and children that I have today and truthfully may not have lived this long to begin with.

» Alec Johannson:
YAS taught me about FAMILY, how to work together as a team, and how to turn weakness into strength. I learned how to GROW in that area.

[Many have spoken about the transformation they made during Showcase, but few talk about how their parents were affected, much less their relationship with them. Imagine your child announcing they are going to go across the country to play in a rock band and share Jesus with people all over the United States! Would you tie them down and call in the rabbi, as Linda Miller's parents tried to do in an earlier story? Many parents called the Showcase office worried their child was getting into a cult, a growing issue among young people during those years. Michael Jones shares a compelling account that many parents, and Showcase vets, can relate to:]

» Michael (Jonesy) Jones (1980-1982):

Boy to Man
My second year I had a band mate, Jimmy Donald (Arceneaux). Jimmy was an only child of a single mother. Frankly, he was a spoiled mama's boy. He wanted to be a guitar player, but because he was carrying a few extra pounds, they made him start as a bass player. When Jimmy would have a rough day, he would call his mom to whine and complain. He ran through his money and then would call his mom to send him more. One day he was on the phone whining to his mom and I asked him if I could talk to her. She asked me, "Is this a cult? They work Jimmy so hard. He doesn't get enough sleep and he always needs money." I assured her that it was not a cult and, yes, we do work hard and we probably don't get enough sleep, but I would look after her son.

You need to understand that I was just Jimmy's bandmate. I did not have authority over him. I was a vet and he was a rookie but for the most part, we were peers. When Jimmy hung up with his mom, I said to him, "Okay, this is how this is going to go. You can no longer call your mom when you're sad. If you want to call your mom, you need to ask me if you are in the right frame of mind and I'll let you know if it's okay. You can no longer ask her for money. You're a man now. Make your money work like all the rest of us do. When you're broke, stop buying things. Don't stay up all night, and get your rest."

He didn't really have to, but he would come to me and ask if he could call his mom. I would say, "Are you sad?" He would say, "No, I'm good." I'd say, "Go ahead and call her." So, fast-forward months later, and I think by this time

Jimmy had moved to the guitar slot. We were playing in his hometown area. We got to meet his proud mama and she said to me, "I gave you my boy and you gave me a man!" It was wonderful for her to be so proud of him, and a little bit funny. I don't want to take credit for this but I do not know where else Jimmy would have gotten this.

In later years, Jimmy was the winner of the prestigious Showcase Award, "Animal of the Year." I was so jealous.

I would not send this without Jimmy's approval. Here is his reply: "Not gonna change a thing—just how I remember it. You are one of the most important men I have ever had in my life—ever. **Love you Mr. Jones, thank you.** I may still be a bit of a mess, but I am God's mess. Thank you for believing in me!"

» TJ Klay (1977-1979):
YAS was my college. I thank God and my wife, Eloise, that I am still a (mostly) full-time musician. There's not a performance I do without a whole bunch of "Lowell's Gold" intertwined.

» Alex Lagos (1983-1984):
I live a just life, as I was taught by my parents. I was a guitar player and became a performer, and when I moved to LA, it helped me stay away from bad things. I eventually started to help others after I became a father, and devoted my life to my kids, who are to this day my best friends and responsible adults.

» Chris Lundquist (1983-1985):
I met my wife in Showcase, and I have always cherished those days of touring with the guys and impacting young lives. We have continued to minister to youth, and especially to other musicians.

» Steve Soderquist (1983-1985):
My work ethic was never the same. Laziness was forever stricken from my life and vocabulary. Anything seemingly insurmountable always brought Lowell's words back to me: Make it happen. Therefore, I did!

» Steve Tharp (1987-1991):
It was like how I imagine boot camp and military service would be. Get up early, fix everything, drive, and make it happen. Lead, follow, or get out of the way... but most of all, "Make it happen!"

» Hiroshi Upshur (1970-1975):
One lesson I learned from Showcase is about perception. Lowell taught me the skunk trick to do during the assembly show. I practiced it to perfection. It

worked. The audience thought I made a real skunk appear. I went out into the audience and the ladies scattered in fear. This showed me that what we think we see is not necessarily true. This applies in life. If one does an investigation into the skunk trick they will find out there is no way I could have had a real skunk. A skunk cannot be tamed. Try approaching a skunk and see what you get. And magic is just that—magic is not real. The Free Fare guys were just regular people up there, but from the audience's perspective we were rock stars, or close to it. I may have looked confident and in control while giving a speech to the assembly show crowd, but deep inside I was nervous and shivering in my boots. What appears is not necessarily so.

Many thanks to Lowell, and to others for the many memories. Showcase was amazing, and I am grateful for the people I met in my travels and got to know because of Showcase. And mostly, I am thankful to God for the experiences.

» Dave Walker (1983-1991):

Showcase became my fraternity, and all my brothers that have come through have and always will remain some of my closest and dearest. God set this path before me. I knew the first time the door opened in the gym that something special was to take place in my life! When you know the path that God sets before you, don't hesitate. Walk boldly in His guidance.

» Linda Miller (1976-1978):

Yes, Yes

[Linda Miller, you may remember, is our groupie convert from Portland. Connie (Watkins) Kolosey reached out to Linda after receiving a letter from her addressed to the Showcase office, and these two young women became long-distance friends. A year or so after God "did a tap dance on her head," Linda received a call from Connie, as the plan God had orchestrated long before began to take shape:]

Connie called to let me know that one of the YAS secretaries was quitting her job because she was having a baby. That left an opening in the office for another secretary, and Connie wondered if I would be interested in coming to Florida and going to work for Showcase. She was sure I would fit in well. I told her that I would have to think about it. I prayed about it, and one week later I was laid off from my job due to budget cuts; God was saying "yes." I packed my bags, said goodbye to family and friends, and headed to Florida, not having the slightest idea of what lay ahead.

One of my main responsibilities as a YAS secretary was to handle the groups' mail and to talk to the group managers every day. One of the managers I talked with daily was Tom Miller. Tom was known as quite the charmer and, true to his reputation, he would use his best flirting skills every time we talked. I fell for it all. In addition, Joe Lathrop (who was the company spiritual director at the time) went out on the road and told Tom all about the new girl in the office. When he got back, he told me all about Tom.

Spring break was coming up. The groups would have some time off and Lowell had planned the inaugural launch of the *Santa Maria* (a replica ship YAS had built for another project) at Snug Harbor. Tom decided to come to the launch (where Connie, Vicky, and I would be serving as hostesses), on the premise of visiting his parents, who lived in St. Pete. He came, we met, and it was pretty much love at first sight. Four months later during rehearsal camp, he proposed—but I said no. How could I marry a guy I had only known for four months and whom my parents had never even met?

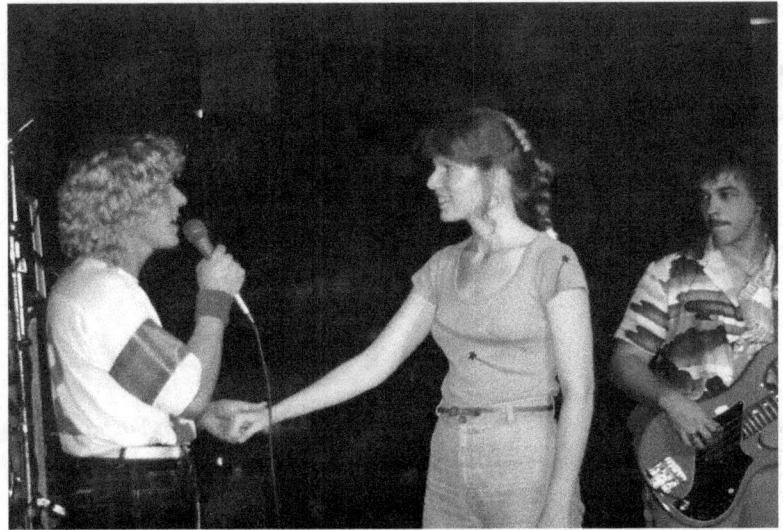

Linda Miller at her first show camp helping Tracey Durant practice "singing to the girl."

A month later when he'd left to go back on the road, I realized I missed him terribly and had made a huge mistake. I called him and said, "If the question is still open, the answer is yes." In true Tom Miller style, he told me the question was no longer open. However, the story ends well with us getting married five months later and hitting the road a week after our wedding. We were managers of Miller Freedom Jam 1, then the next year, Miller Free Fare and Miller Freedom Jam 2. Then, Tom took over the booking department at the home office, and the rest is history.

I can't thank Lowell enough for providing the way for God to grab my heart and completely change my life. Because of Young American Showcase, I accepted Jesus, Connie and I have been best friends for over forty years. As of this writing, Tom and I have been married forty-two years and have built a wonderful family.

[Linda and Tom, Connie and Gary were two among many couples owing their relationship to Lowell's amazing experiment. Here's one more love story, in which Tom Miller played a pivotal role:]

» Paul Turner (1976-1978):

How to Catch a Journalism Major

Tom Miller was an extraordinary manager. Saying that, I hope most of us had "the best manager ever," but Tom earnestly cared about his guys—and didn't mind showing it. Whether our need was nutritional, informational, spiritual, or otherwise, he was there for us. It was the "otherwise" that got my attention.

My first year I was with the "Miller Free Fare" and we traveled from Virginia up to New Hampshire my first few months. From day one, he told our band all about Kim and Leslie. They were both great gals and would make somebody a wonderful catch, and he wasn't talking about fishing! They were both young Christian gals he had met the previous year on tour with a different Showcase group. Kim lived in Colorado and liked horses. That's all I remember about Kim, but I do remember a lot about Leslie.

Leslie Tudor went to Westerville High School and had written a song that St. Jude's Children's Research Hospital adopted as their national theme song. She received an award for this accomplishment about the same time Tom's band was traveling through town, so the principal used the opportunity to surprise Leslie and recognize her in front of the high school body. He did not realize the choral director had selected Leslie to introduce the band that morning. Of course, she accepted the award and, still in a state of shock, had to immediately step up to the mike to introduce the band—only, she could not remember the band's name, even though it was stenciled in large letters on the speaker stacks. The students shouted "Free Fare" repeatedly to help her out, probably the best intro any band has every gotten. Needless to say, Tom realized she was a special young lady and stayed in touch with her.

The following year, I was in Tom's band when the schools in the Boston area closed because of harsh weather and a national fuel shortage. After a few days in a large Howard Johnson's motel, we headed down to St. Pete to regroup with another Showcase band who had been traveling in the Ohio region. Seizing the opportunity, Tom charted a course from our Boston motel to St. Pete "directly" through Westerville, Ohio. Leslie, now attending Ohio State, was to meet us at a local Bill Knapp's restaurant. On the way, I came down with the flu, losing my stomach continually in the small, carpeted compartment of our step van.

We were late and hungry by the time we reached the restaurant, so everybody quickly and excitedly jumped out of the van and ran inside—everybody, that is, except for Bil Curry and me. Bil was engaged to a girl back in Harrisburg, and not interested in meeting Leslie. I was interested, but in no shape to meet anybody. After about twenty minutes, I forced myself to "make it happen." I threw on my fringe leather jacket and made it inside. My bandmates were all seated with Leslie around a large round table. She had already passed out gifts to each one. Tom got a Michael O'Martian "White Horse" cassette and each of "us" got a recently published copy of the NIV New Testament. It was all I could do to present myself well. Despite the flu surging through my veins, I couldn't help but notice that this was the sweetest, warmest girl I had ever laid eyes on. Everyone was finishing their meal when I arrived, so very soon we said goodbye and hit the road again. Before we left, we took a couple pictures to remember the moment.

Left: Paul Turner, Leslie Tudor, Gary Kolosey, Bil Curry (back). **Right:** Leslie with Tom Miller.

So how does a guy catch a journalism major? He writes her letters. He "earns the right to be heard." He "makes it happen."

He starts by telling her what he thought of meeting her. Then he writes about himself. His background, beliefs, hopes, daily events, and so on. He just keeps writing. And with many hours on the road to the next gig, there is plenty of time to write.

Days pass. Weeks pass. Months go by and I write many letters. Let's call it daily. Eventually, she writes back. Then, she plans a trip to St. Pete to visit the Showcase offices and consider a position there. Ultimately, she decides to continue her education instead, but she starts to fall for this guy who has faithfully written dozens of letters to catch her eye and capture her heart. We still have those letters. In 2021, we celebrated being married forty-two years. Someday, I'm going to read those letters again.

Within the last several years, Leslie has coauthored, edited, and published many books, one of which is Lowell Lytle's story, *Diving into the Deep*. She also wove together these Showcase stories. In a very real way, she got her "Showcase position" after all.

PART EIGHT

THE WRAP

Lowell: Dare to touch the bull's horns.

So, after all those years, what did Young American Showcase actually accomplish? The scientific answer is, we do not know. We cannot measure it. We cannot track it. We cannot prove it. Does that mean it didn't happen? Does that mean it accomplished nothing? Far from it! How do we know? We have eyewitness accounts from people who were there, testimonies that are consistent with each other, unscripted, without agenda, far more than have been shared here. Below, one of the original members, Joe Brown, succinctly sums up this radical experiment in evangelism. Following that, we found some common threads to examine.

Was it all worth it? What do you think?

The first group at the Seidelman farm. Wayne Hackett, Joe Brown, Terry Casburn, Gary Horton (missing: Lowell Lytle)

» Joe Brown (1969-1972):

The Young American Showcase mission was about spreading the gospel, and to a certain extent Lowell's desired goal was fulfilled. Many kids indicated they had prayed with us and accepted Christ as their personal Savior. Who knows how many of those planted seeds sprouted? Who knows what effects still ripple through the lives and families of those kids who heard Free Fare? Only Heaven knows. I think all YAS veterans hope someday to find out just how many lives we touched. Perhaps in the next world, someone will approach each of us and say, "I want to thank you for what you did when you came to our school. It changed my life forever. I am here because of what you did."

Perhaps just as important was the ministry to the YAS musicians themselves. Many came to Showcase from bands who played some pretty seedy lounges and clubs, where less than positive influences held sway. For many of those young men, YAS was quite literally a Godsend—a place where they could share their talents in bands with high performance standards, doing entertaining shows with great sound and lighting, and—even better—with the greatest message they could possibly deliver. What an honor and privilege.

And with role models like Lowell Lytle, who believed that God would "make it happen" as long as we were moving and taking action to overcome barriers, and Gary Horton, who constantly taught us Biblical truths, and Lowell's wife, Barbara, our surrogate office mother while we were on the road, and the YAS bookers, some of whom became our father confessors while on the road, how could we help but grow, at least a little.

We agree with Joe. One of the reasons we wanted to examine more closely the impact Showcase had on participants' lives is because we observed that a very high number of Showcase vets and former staffers became pastors or church planters, founded their own ministries, served in their local church, or in other ways took on significant ministry leadership roles in order to continue reaching people with the gospel. Many from the Showcase family continued their music or entertainment careers and are performing to this day. A surprising number reached national or international success. Those that entered other fields quite often were elevated to positions of leadership, and all would agree their Showcase training weighed heavily in both their career path and level of success. In researching this book, we originally hoped to find the "secret sauce" that made such a difference in their lives.

One Showcase vet lamented, "Isn't just trying to live your life like Christ enough?" This honest question revealed the tendency we have to only recognize the grandest accomplishments, as if anyone who settled down, got a "real" job, and lived a simple, God-honoring life was wasting their experience or talents. So, let's be clear. Only God decides for each of us, individually, what is "enough." We are not about comparing lives, and we cannot scientifically prove any specific cause and effect Young American Showcase had, or may still have to this day. We know that we are not getting the full story, that there are members who so love and revere the founder of YAS they will never speak ill of their experience. But, we can look at the first-hand testimony we have received, the first-hand shared experience, and listen, find common threads, and draw some observational conclusions. We can hope that doing so might motivate future generations to answer their calling, try something extraordinary, and come up with their own radical experiment. We can encourage leaders struggling to move their people forward by sharing the timeless principles of leadership gleaned from the Showcase experience. We can remind those who were changed by Showcase that they are not done yet. That is our purpose.

So, what were the common threads?

Consistency

1. **Consistency in leadership.** Leaders were unwavering and consistent in their standards and expectations. They were united in their relationship with each other, and held each other to the same high standards as their bands.
2. **Consistency in method.** Everything from how the truck was packed, to timing, to showmanship, to the format was the same from group to group. Set lists had little variation. Variation from the method was not tolerated. The rules were the same for everyone on the road. The high performance standards, behavior expectations, responsibilities on the road, were fair and challenging.
3. **Consistency in message.** The talk at the end of the night show varied by speaker as it often included a personal experience, but always contained the same basic elements. The message sent through band members' behavior, in how they were treated by their managers, in how company leadership treated everyone, was consistent.

Mentorship (aka discipleship)

1. Managers mentored band members. More than being in charge, they paid attention to spiritual growth and stability, mental health, physical health, relationship growth, and personal maturity. The manager took care of them, or helped them take care of themselves. As the group quickly became a road family, the manager was the "dad."
2. Veteran band members mentored rookies. Often the first to see when a rookie needed guidance or a quick correction, they were the "older

brothers" who set them straight before "dad" stepped in. (They also had their brotherly fun.)
3. The home office team mentored everyone. A spiritual director sometimes came out on the road to help, as well as the critique team, which sometimes included Lance and/or Lowell. They might come out to straighten up the show, or attitudes, or make personnel changes. Many Showcase vets looked at Lowell as a father figure, imposing, but someone who they knew loved and cared for them.

Mission

1. Every band went on the road for the same reason—to win the souls of a generation back from the cultural traps of the day and point them to Jesus. Every band member bought into this mission, even though, on a personal level, they wanted and loved the road experience, the performance growth, the adrenaline. The mission is what drove them to leave it all on the gym floor every show. They lived their mission every hour of every day.
2. Bands were taught to "earn the right to be heard" through love and energy, and in every sense, love and energy permeated the entire organization, from the top leadership, the home office, the managers, and the band members.
3. Every band member made great sacrifices to be on the road, as did managers, bookers, everyone in the organization. As someone aptly pointed out, no one got rich in this crazy endeavor. Without a mission they fully believed in, there would be no willingness to make great sacrifice, to set aside egos and work together as a team for a common goal.

In addition to these common threads, throughout this story we have identified specific leadership keystones, and certainly the "methods to the madness" we uncovered are timeless and effective for any organization. The truth is this: you cannot put the power of God's blessing in a bottle. You cannot prescribe a short list of laws, rules, and mantras to a ministry or business and expect the same result. What happened with this radical experiment in evangelism called Young American Showcase had so many variables, so many obstacles, so many ways it could have failed—there was no "secret sauce." There is just this: when God's hand is on it, when you are obedient to the Holy Spirit's call on your life, when you stay humble but courageous, when you stay in the Word and surround yourself with people who will keep you accountable, you put yourself in a position where God can use you. You put your rudder in the water. Hold on. It's going to be quite a ride.

A CALL TO ACTION

FROM LOWELL LYTLE

Lowell Lytle, November 2021

The year was around 1940. I was about eight years of age and every summer my father would pack up the car with all kinds of camping equipment—a large tent, a heavy rope, fishing poles, etc.—and we would go camping and fishing for two weeks at a time at Little Wolf Lake, which was southeast of Jackson, Michigan, my hometown.

My father was always careful when it came to finding the right spot to pitch the tent. He would make sure the land was level. Then he would dig a ditch completely around the tent to catch any rainwater. Then he would completely encircle the tent with that heavy rope. I asked him, "Why do you do that?"

He said, "That's to stop the snakes from coming in." He explained, "Snakes will not go over that scratchy rope." I thought my father was very clever.

The best fishing time is usually in the morning, so every morning, my whole family—my mother, father, brother Terry, and I would pack into a rented wooden boat and my father would row us out to our favorite fishing hole. When we would arrive, I remember my mother always saying, "Don't shuffle your feet. The fish will hear you. And whatever you do, ease the anchor in the water slowly. Don't throw the anchor overboard. It will make a big splash and you will scare the fish."

The fish that I always liked to catch and eat were perch and bluegills; they were tasty. My dad, however, seemed to always catch a dogfish. They're ugly looking and you can't eat them, but boy, do they ever put up a big fight. I remember one time my father caught one, and it was so big that it broke his cane pole in two. When we would arrive back to shore, Dad would always throw the dogfish in the garbage can. After the first week, all the campers called us the Dogfish Lytles.

Don't throw the anchor overboard

My mother always liked to fish, and so did I. I still do. She led me to Christ when I was seven years of age, and the next morning when the mailman or the milkman came to our house, she gave me the Gospel of John or a tract to give to them. She was trying to make an evangelist out of me, and it worked! Jesus said, "I will make you fishers of men. Go into all the world and preach the gospel to every creature." What is the gospel? It is the true story of the death, burial, and resurrection of Jesus Christ. Those who will put their faith and trust in Him and ask Him to come into their lives, they will have eternal life. (John 3:16)

That is the most important message that God ever gave to mankind! And we as Christians have kept it the most guarded secret. We have hidden it behind stained-glass windows, steeples, and choir robes, and we have put our churches in the middle of graveyards, with tombstones all around, playing music on an organ that they play at funerals, then we ask the world, "Wouldn't you like to join us?" It's time for us to get relevant. We are ambassadors for Jesus Christ in a world that belongs to Satan. God does not allow the angels to tell the story because they wouldn't know how to begin. They don't have blood running through their veins like we do.

Christ wants *us* to be fishers of men. But you don't go fishing with a bare hook; that scares the fish. You need the bait, and you need it on the hook. In 1970, young people were biting on rock and roll. That wasn't my kind of music. I played trombone in a big band in 1948. That was my style of music! But, it was time to go fishing! The apostle Paul said, "I become all things to all people so that by all possible means I might save some" (1 Corinthians 9:22). That sounds a little deceitful. However, the apostle Paul also said in 2 Corinthians 12:16 "I caught you with guile" (KJV). In the Webster's dictionary, the word "guile" is translated as "deceit." Other Bible versions say "trickery." I call it bait.

In 1967, I used magic and ventriloquism as bait. In Fort Myers, Florida, I did a high school assembly show with magic and ventriloquism. I invited everyone to go to a different place the following night to see a whole new show. One hundred fifty kids from Fort Myers High School came to that show.

Lowell using his "bait" of magic, 1967 at a Pizza Panic, Florida.

I did a magic trick illustrating the gospel, and I gave an invitation for those who would like to receive Christ to do so that night. Sixty-five of them responded to the invitation. I realized right then I was fishing where the fish were.

In 1968, Gary Horton and I started young American Showcase. Deceit, trickery, call it what you will, but it works. Ask God to enlighten you to new ideas, but whatever you do, ease the anchor in. Don't throw it. You'll make a big splash and scare the fish.

EPILOGUE: GOD'S ROCK AND ROLL ARMY

Young American Showcase was revolutionary, for both the ten-plus million students who shared the experience of seeing a band play their school, and for the hundreds of musicians, managers, trainers, bookers, administrators, and leaders who altered their life's direction to play a part in this radical experiment. YAS changed parents, schools, and communities. It transformed hearts, minds, and more than a million souls by the most conservative estimate.

This one last story captures so much of the components that pulled everything together: the element of surprise, the team working hard to earn the right to be heard, the discipline, training, leadership, and the love and energy that purchased a young man's soul.

» Mike Yocum (1975–1976, 1979):

In 1972, I was seventeen years old and a senior in a parochial high school. My love of playing music was rapidly developing; I'd been playing since I was fifteen and dreaming of it long before that. I was in a band with friends from high school and we got to play at dances in our student center.

One day, roughly three months into our school year, we were called down to our gymnasium for an assembly. No one knew what the assembly was for; however, as I entered I saw that a PA and instruments were set up. Now, this looked interesting! The students were buzzing with anticipation when the announcer said, "From St. Petersburg, Florida, Free Fare!" A seven-piece band with three horn players took the stage and proceeded to impress me thoroughly. I could tell that the guys in the band weren't much older than I was. They were much better than any young band I had ever seen. The forty-five-minute program flew by and we were all invited back for a night show, which of course I attended. It was great again, musical, engaging, and even funny at times. At the end of the show that evening, the front man announced that he and the band were Christians. Christians! If there was anything that didn't mix with rock and roll as it had been presented to me, it was Christianity. It gave me a lot to think about. I asked the president of the student council if he would give me the address of the organization, which was called Young American Showcase. I wrote for and received information, but didn't act on it just then.

Two years later, I had been majoring in music at our local community college. I was at the home of the girl I was dating, and her little sister came in and announced that there had been a band at their school called Free Fare, and that they were having a night show. I dragged my girlfriend to it. It was indeed Free Fare; however, all but one of the guys were different. It was another great show, and afterward I asked the manager of the band for company information again. This time, I applied.

It had become clear to me that my friends in my band, whom I loved, did not share the same goals as me. All I wanted to do was play, and I thought that playing with such a professional organization could only help me. After a rigorous application process carried on by mail and over the phone, I was accepted for rehearsal camp in July 1975. Lance Abair, the company talent coordinator, warned me that if I went through with this, I would never be the same. As I would discover, he was right.

Top: Mike Yocum; Middle: Rosco Cooper, Bubba Copeland, Marty Wright; Bottom: Kim Bjornson, Phil Hardley (manager).

Rehearsal camp was a blur of the hard work of putting a show together, Christian doctrine and fellowship, entertainment concepts, and rapid growth. The band I was placed in had five guys: a two-year veteran, a one-year veteran, and three rookies (including me). We toured Virginia, New York, Pennsylvania, Ohio, and Ontario. For the 1975–76 school year, we worked hard, sometimes doing seven shows in a day. It was exhausting, but satisfying; it was everything I'd wanted. Our manager was a former youth pastor who had a solid doctrinal background. Before our night shows, we would get together for a half hour devotional. Not only was I growing musically, I was growing spiritually.

I didn't realize it at the time, however in many ways the Showcase experience was like stepping through the looking glass. When I stepped out again after that year was over, life at home was never the same. I saw things differently. I heard music differently. I had grown spiritually. In short, I was a different person.

Although I tried hard to meld back in with my old friends, those relationships were never the same.

I toured once more in the first half of 1979. The company was putting together an experimental band to play smaller schools, and they wanted a veteran to join the playing manager and two rookies. I left my home and my friends once again, knowing this would be the last time I would tour, in all likelihood. Again, touring was intense but satisfying. A highlight of that tour was visiting Nova Scotia, where no Showcase band had been to date.

When I returned home after that tour, my friends, including my girlfriend, wanted nothing to do with me. Looking back, as painful as it was, I believe that the Lord was gently guiding me toward a new life, one with Him at the center, on the throne.

I owe Showcase a debt I cannot repay. I met some of the finest people I've ever encountered. A young musician's dream of touring and playing to audiences that actually wanted to see you came true. I grew physically, mentally, spiritually—and musically. I experienced magic moments sharing the gospel with people; a brotherhood. A rock and roll army.

Remember what I said earlier about Christianity and rock and roll not mixing? It turns out they can, beautifully.

Mike Yocum present day. Photo credit: Crystal Prahl

DO YOU REMEMBER?

As you read this book and enjoyed the photos, you may remember a group coming to your school. You may even still have a poster rolled up in the attic, or a photo album with some mementos to share. We would love to hear from you! Connect with us on social media:

- Visit our Facebook Page: https://fb.me/GodsRockandRollArmy
- Send a message: https://m.me/GodsRockandRollArmy

As time goes on, we will add more photos and other media to this site, so follow us!

- Find the book trailer at the Encourage Publishing YouTube channel: https://www.youtube.com/channel/UC-rhqdV09aymXcOHxTps0qA

You may be a long-lost Showcase member who has yet to reconnect with your Showcase family. They miss you! Join the private Facebook group, "Showcase Veterans" and feel the love.

WOULD YOU HELP?

We would love to know how this book impacted your life. Your feedback helps us improve and continue to tell meaningful, uplifting stories. There are several easy ways you can help.

- **Leave an honest review** on Amazon or your favorite book review site. Your review is extremely important and deeply appreciated.
- Leave a comment on any of our social media sites, or send us an email: info@encouragebooks.com

ACKNOWLEDGMENTS

God's Rock and Roll Army was a story that has been told over the past three decades by the people who lived it, one story at a time. The people of Showcase formed an indelible bond over their shared experience, a common thread that existed even if they participated at different times, in different bands or capacities. Stories were shared over coffee, over dinner, through social media, by email and phone, in photos, audio and video recordings, and written word. Members of this improbable club gathered, in large groups and small, with family and friends, trying to explain what happened to them, and through them. But outside of the Showcase family, no one could truly understand. Nobody could completely believe it. Yet, it happened. It's still happening, as a matter of fact.

Most of the paper trail that Showcase left has been lost, but the stories continue. For many years, a handful of people worked to provide a place on social media where Showcasers could connect and leave their memories. They gathered photographs, and organized a large reunion in 2007 and again in 2022. Smaller reunions regularly take place organically, all over the country. This book is, in no small part, only possible because of those efforts, and only manages to capture a small portion of the experience.

Now, as I acknowledge the following people, imagine them running out on stage in full Michael Braun regalia, graciously accepting applause, as Lance Abair taught them. If any fail to receive my gratitude joyfully, be sure to throw some rolled up socks at them.

Connie and Gary Kolosey! This book would not have come to pass without the tireless work of Connie and Gary. Thank you for all you have sacrificed for the Showcase family across the decades, and particularly for your work bringing this book to life.

Paul Turner! A special thank you to my husband, Paul. First, for saying yes to Showcase all those years ago, and for embodying the love of Jesus for me for the past forty-three years and counting. Your support is truly what made this book happen.

The contributing writers! We must acknowledge those whose thorough and thoughtful writing contributions added immeasurable texture and validity to this story, and supported our mission of inspiring a new generation to try new radical experiments in evangelism. Truly, the time is short. To those wonderful writers, named throughout the book, we extend our deep gratitude. You are all a personal encouragement to me.

The extended Showcase family! The band members, home office staff, management, you all are heroes to me. The term "hero" sometimes feels diluted, used in almost any circumstance. In the world's eyes, your work and sacrifice during your years with Young American Showcase may not be given a second thought, but from an eternal perspective, you more than earned the title of "hero." You gave countless people the keys to eternal security. I was never on staff with Showcase, yet, my life has been immeasurably altered because of you and, by extension, so have my children's lives. I met my dear husband, Paul, through Showcase. I found my calling, my life's work, and my mission because of Showcase, and because one beloved man, Lowell Lytle, led the way. I am forever indebted. You are all heroes, every one of you, and I am grateful for you, no matter the role you played, nor the time you spent. Thank you.

Gary Horton! Thank you for always knowing when to give me a call, for listening when God put me on your heart, and for your prayers. Whenever I heard your voice, I knew we were going to be fine. Most importantly, thank you for your lifelong work spreading the gospel and helping generations raise the bar.

Lowell Lytle! So much has already been said about you, and I know it all makes you very uncomfortable. So, let me just add, getting to know you in this stage of your life over the past decade has made me a better person. I am so privileged to have had this opportunity. Your willingness to be vulnerable and honest, your enthusiasm, encouragement, your example, your friendship, mean everything to me. You know I love you. As the apostle Paul said to the Philippians, so I say to you:

> "I thank my God every time I remember you. In all my prayers for...you, I always pray with joy because of your partnership in the gospel from the first day until now, being confident of this, that he who began a good work in you will carry it on to completion until the day of Christ Jesus. It is right for me to feel this way about you, since I have you in my heart..." (Philippians 1:3–7 NIV)

ABOUT THE AUTHOR

Prior to *God's Rock and Roll Army*, Leslie Turner cowrote *Diving into the Deep* (2014, Encourage Publishing). Leslie is also nationally published as a contributing writer in several books and magazines, and has two blogs:

- The Power of SMALL: Smart Tips for Storytellers
- The Power of CHANGE, the Mercies of FAITH

Leslie Turner is the owner and founder of Encourage Publishing, an independent hybrid book publishing company established in 2014. She holds two degrees from Indiana University, and currently serves on two national editorial boards: the National Association of Student Financial Aid Administrators, and the Independent Book Publishers Association.

Her next book will be an inspirational biography that tells the stories of several "ordinary" people who overcame extraordinary challenges, expected publication early 2024. "We are surrounded by people everywhere we go who are walking heroes, but you would never know it. I love telling their stories and inspiring those whose struggles may seem invisible to everyone else, but never to God. I do have a novel I am anxious to write," she notes. "With the working title *Helen of Antioch*, it's going to be a historical fiction based loosely on the teenage journals of a woman near and dear to my heart who was born in the early twentieth century, and passed away in 2010." You can follow Leslie on social media or through Encourage Publishing, www.encouragepublishing.com.

Encourage Publishing exclusively publishes carefully curated works that lead to positive change, or encourage the world in an uplifting way. Their titles inspire, inform, educate, entertain, and motivate without tearing anyone down along the way. Their mission is: *To tell your story and conduct our business in a way that honors Christ and encourages others. Every day we positively change our world!*

Lowell Lytle and Gary Horton, 2021. At publication, Lowell will have celebrated his ninetieth birthday. Gary celebrated eighty years in September 2021.

BONUS: A BEAUTIFUL STORY

FROM GARY HORTON

Many years ago, I was asked at a youth camp about Barabbas, the criminal that was up for the death penalty with Jesus. So, I did some homework and I realized that there was something interesting about his name.

Pontius Pilate, the governor, came up with a cop-out as to what he was going to do with Jesus, because he knew that Jesus was not guilty. This kangaroo court was forcing him to make a decision, so he asked the crowd.

Every time the governor had this kind of a situation, the people were allowed by law to make the decision for him. Barabbas had been given a death sentence because he was a murderer. Jesus had not broken any laws. Pilate gave the crowd a choice. "Who do you want me to turn loose, Barabbas the criminal, or Jesus, the so-called Messiah?"

The crowd asked for Barabbas.

Picture Barabbas. He was so much like we are as sinners. We are condemned. We are born physically alive, but we are dead spiritually. We are the enemy of Almighty God, because of sin. And so, Barabbas is a picture of us. His name, "bar Abba," means "son of the father." "Bar" means "son of," and "Abba" means "the father." Here we are, sons and daughters of *our* fathers, our human fathers, which puts us in a situation where we are spiritually dead, born with a sinful nature. We are enemies of the cross. We are enemies of Almighty God, and we deserve the death penalty, just like Barabbas did! But he was set free, because the perfect man, the perfect Savior, the Redeemer, took his place. Jesus took the beating, the crucifixion, and the hatred of the crowd. They hated Him without reason. He was the perfect Son of God! But God allowed Jesus Christ, who knew no sin, to become sin for us that day, that we might become the righteousness of God through Him. So, we are born of our human father that gave to us a sin nature, and we are condemned under that. We deserve the death penalty just like Barabbas. But somebody took our place. He was the Son of God, in other words, the Son of the Father—bar Abba. Barabbas. The crowd yelled for the criminal Barabbas to be set free, but it was all a part of God's plan that the Son of the Father would take the place of all of us that day.

We become the Barabbas of our day; we are the criminals. We are the ones who deserve the death penalty. But just like Jesus took Barabbas's place while Barabbas was set free, Jesus took our place. He took my place. He took your place. He took the place of the human race. God was willing to put His own Son on death row to die for the sins of the world, and for ALL of us who are like Barabbas. How strategic that during the trial of Christ they offered a man named Barabbas to take His place. Barabbas was set free, and the world asked for the condemnation of the Son of God, even though we are the sons of sin, the sons of condemnation. We were born spiritually dead. Just because we are physically alive does not mean we are set right. But all of a sudden, the sons and daughters of the fathers, you and me, have been so blessed, because somebody took our place on death row. We can live because he died in our place.

The beautiful part is that Jesus came back from the dead. The gospel is the death, burial, and *resurrection*, and who ever calls upon His name and believes that Christ died for his sins, that He was buried where you and I should have been buried, that He rose again because He *is* everlasting life, that person has been freed! That person will also have everlasting life! *You, sentenced to death like Barabbas, can be freed!* Jesus was the Son of God that took the place of sons and daughters of the human race. We were *all* under the curse of Barabbas. I don't know the rest of the story of Barabbas, whether he came to know the Savior or not. I would think he would stick around just to see who that man was who was allowed to take his place on death row. "Why was I allowed to be set free, when I was the guilty one?" This is a question we should all be asking. "Why would Jesus do something like that for me? Why would His Father allow it?" The answer is in John 3:16: "For God so loved the world that he gave his one and only son, that whoever believes in him shall not perish but have eternal life" (NIV). *That's it.* That's the *reason*. He loves you. He loves me.

You see, that's the beautiful story of the grace of our Almighty God. I am a better man now because I know the King of glory. The man Jesus Christ, who lives in me and removes the condemnation of my sins, has given me the righteousness of God, and I am blessed forever. How thankful I am that God found a way to include me in His grace and mercy.

WHAT DID YOU DO WITH YOUR TICKET?

Throughout this book, we have been talking about the tickets the bands would collect at the end of each night show from students who either accepted the Lord that night or who wanted to know more. You may have been one of those students all those years ago who saw a show. What did you do with your ticket?

You may be a long-time churchgoer, even a student of the Bible, but perhaps you never really understood this simple truth about a relationship with Jesus before. You have knowledge about it, but have never actually accepted the gift of salvation. Or, perhaps you have always known about it, but never believed, never asked Jesus into your heart to be your Lord and Savior. It's not too late to turn in your ticket! If you would, pray this prayer right now:

> "Dear Lord, I know that I am a sinner. I believe that You died on the cross for my sins, and that You rose from the dead! I ask You to come into my heart to save me from my sin and be Lord and Master of my life. Help me to live for You! Thank you, Lord, for saving my soul!"

Amen! If you prayed that prayer in faith, you are saved! Your place in Heaven is certain! You are set free! As soon as you can, tell someone. Get a Bible and start learning about your new life of freedom. Your journey has just begun.

If you just prayed that prayer, or if you have more questions, contact us. We've included some "tickets" in the back of this book. Cut one off if you like, write your name, address, and email on the back, and send it to us with a note telling us where you are in your faith journey. We will send you something to help you along.

Mail your tickets to Encourage Publishing at 1116 Creekview Circle, New Albany, Indiana 47150. Reading an ebook? Email us: info@encouragebooks.com.

LAFF-OUT

ADMIT ONE

NEW SHOW
HOUR & A HALF
FEATURING
THE "FREE FARE"

$1.50

Mail to: Encourage Publishing
God's Rock and Roll Army
1116 Creekview Circle
New Albany, IN 47150
Or email to: info@encouragebooks.com

FREE FARE

NEW SHOW
HOUR & A HALF
ADMIT ONE

$1.50

Mail to: Encourage Publishing
God's Rock and Roll Army
1116 Creekview Circle
New Albany, IN 47150 or email to: info@encouragebooks.com

PIZZA PANIC

ADMIT ONE / MAGIC SHOW

PIZZA......ALL YOU CAN EAT......WITH ICE COLD POP...& A 45 MIN. MAGIC SHOW......FEATURING PROFESSIONAL COMIC MAGICIAN AND VENTRILOQUIST....
LOWELL LYTLE
ST. PETERSBURG, FLA.

Mail to: Encourage Pubishing
God's Rock and Roll Army
1116 Creekview Circle
New Albany, IN 47150, Or email to: info@encouragebooks.com

ADMIT ONE
$1.00

"Freedom Jam"

Mail to: Encourage Pubishing
God's Rock and Roll Army
1116 Creekview Circle
New Albany, IN 47150
or email to: info@encouragebooks.com

This page intentionally left blank

www.ingramcontent.com/pod-product-compliance
Lightning Source LLC
Chambersburg PA
CBHW071959070526
44583CB00015B/1256